RANDY CHARLES EPPING

A BEGINNER'S GUIDE

TO THE WORLD

ECONOMY

Randy Charles Epping, an American citizen currently living in Zurich, Switzerland, has worked in international finance for several years, holding management positions in European and American investment banks in Geneva, London, and Zurich. He holds a master's degree in international finance from Yale University. In addition, he has received a master's degree from the University of Paris–Sorbonne, and a bachelor's degree from the University of Notre Dame. He is the managing director of IFS Project Management A.G., a Swiss-based international consulting company. Mr. Epping is fluent in six languages: English, French, German, Italian, Portuguese, and Spanish.

A BEGINNER'S GUIDE
TO THE
WORLD ECONOMY

A BEGINNER'S GUIDE TO THE

WORLD ECONOMY

Seventy-Seven Basic Economic
Concepts That Will Change
the Way You See the World

RANDY CHARLES EPPING

VINTAGE BOOKS
A DIVISION OF RANDOM HOUSE, INC.
NEW YORK

SECOND VINTAGE BOOKS EDITION, NOVEMBER 1995

Copyright © 1992, 1995 by Randy Charles Epping

Maps used on pages xviii and xix, based on maps in the *New State of the World Atlas*, 5th edition, by Michael Kidron and Ronald Seagal, copyright © 1995 by Myriad Editions Limited, London.

Library of Congress Cataloging-in-Publication Data
Epping, Randy Charles.
A beginner's guide to the world economy : seventy-seven basic economic concepts that will change the way you see the world / Randy Charles Epping.—2nd ed.
p.   cm.
ISBN 0-679-76440-2
1. International finance.   2. Finance.   I. Title.
HG3881.E573   1995
337—dc20   95-18498
CIP

Design by Robert Bull Design

Manufactured in the United States of America
10 9 8 7 6 5 4 3 2 1

If economists want to be understood, let them use plainer words . . . [and] address those words less to politicians and more to everybody else. Politicians care about what voters think, especially voters in blocks, and not a shred about what economists think. Talking to politicians about economics is therefore a waste of time. The only way to make governments behave as if they were economically literate is to confront them with electorates that are.

The Economist

This book is dedicated to Jim Ragsdale. I would also like to thank everyone who helped along the way—in particular, Janos Farago in Geneva and Emanuele Pignatelli in Zurich (without whose help this book would really not have been possible) and Chuck Painter, who first inspired me to write this book. A special thanks to all those who helped with ideas and suggestions, making this book as "user friendly" as possible: Shawn Engelberg of Lake Oswego, Oregon; Del Franz of New York City; Otto Bohlman of New Haven, Connecticut; Paul Barichman of Athens, Georgia; Rodrigo Fiães of Rio de Janeiro; Joanna Hurley of Albuquerque; Gary Epping of Portland, Oregon; Elemer Hantos of Nyon, Switzerland; Robert Malley of Washington, D.C.; Pedro and Marisa Moreira Salles of São Paulo; Terry Ragsdale of New York; Jean-Marc and Virginia Pilpoul of Paris; Sebastian Velasco of Madrid; Alex Neuman of Zurich; Rich Rimer of Amsterdam; Enrique Schmid of San Pedro Sula; Benoit Demeulemeester of Zurich; Anders Thomsen of Copenhagen; Chris Elliott of Geneva; Tom Header of New York; Persio Arida of São Paulo; and Michael Piore at MIT in Cambridge, Massachusetts. I would also like to thank my editors at Vintage Books—Marty Asher, for his vision and confidence in developing and publishing this book as a Vintage Original, and Edward Kastenmeier, for his tireless efforts in the preparation of this new edition. Finally, a special thanks to all the readers who contacted me in Zurich (Internet: 100561.3462 @compuserve.com) with comments and suggestions, making this new edition an even better guide to the expanding global economy.

CONTENTS

INTRODUCTION

An explosion in the world economy has taken place in the years since this book was first published. Many new countries and economies have been created, trade wars have broken out, trade blocks have been formed, and an increasing number of jobs have become dependent on global markets.

Every day, it seems, we hear more and more about the global economy. Phrases like "economic sanctions," "24-hour global trading," and "free-trade agreements" appear regularly in our newspapers and magazines and on television.

Whether we are willing to admit it or not, the world economy has become an integral factor in our daily lives. From the imported alarm clock that wakes us up in the morning to our retirement and college funds being invested abroad while we sleep at night, our lives are increasingly influenced by this new animal called the "World Economy." Whoever we are—environmentalists or business people, homemakers or college students—we need to understand the basics of the world economy if we are to be effective citizens and consumers.

The first step is to become economically literate. For many of us, however, the study of economics has been an exercise in futility, full of obscure graphs and equations, and hopelessly out of touch with our daily lives. This doesn't have to be the case.

In fact, the world economy is really no more complicated than the domestic economy we experience every day. We don't think twice about crossing the street to deposit our money in a bank that gives a better interest rate than the one next door. In an expanding global economy, we shouldn't think twice about crossing borders to invest our money or sell our goods and services.

By understanding the basics of the world economy, we can begin to make better political and economic decisions; and with economically literate voters pushing them on, our politicians will start making more rational economic decisions, leading to a more prosperous and perhaps even more environmentally sound world in the years to come.

This is not a "get-rich-quick" book. If you want to make a fortune in international finance, you will have to look elsewhere. However, it is important to understand the basics before undertaking any investment, so this book could be a great first step to any profitable venture into the global financial marketplace.

Many of the comments and suggestions I received after publishing the first edition of this book have been incorporated into this edition. Readers of the first edition frequently cited the book as instrumental in their first steps in the global marketplace—as investors, policy makers, or successful international entrepreneurs. Understanding the basics is always a useful first step in any new venture, and this is certainly the case in the often confusing world of international trade and finance.

This book is meant to be fun and accessible. It was fun to write and it should never stop being fun to read. No graphs or equations are used, and statistics are always accompanied by examples to give meaning to the numbers. *A Beginner's Guide to the World Economy,* as the name implies, covers only the basics. The complicated economic theories and principles will be left to others.

Although it may be useful to start with the general economic concepts found at the beginning of the book, each section can be read individually. These sections can be read from front to back, from back to front, or at random. The glossary at the end can be used for quick reference in the future, when unfamiliar terms reappear in the news or come up in daily conversation.

Remember, the world economy can be easily understood. Once we have understood the basics, the global economy can become a great adventure, where foreign lands and peoples interact in fascinating ways. It just needs to be simply explained. Enjoy it!

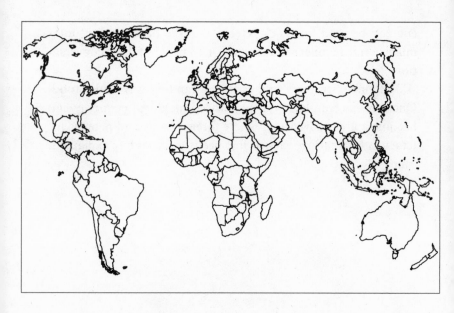

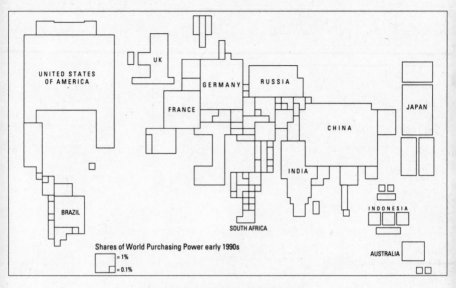

PURCHASING POWER

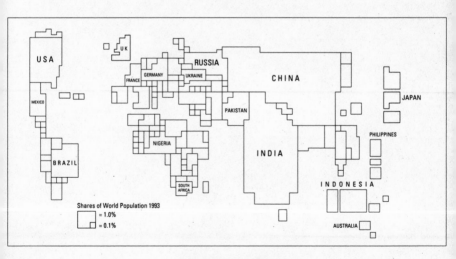

POPULATION

A BEGINNER'S GUIDE
TO THE
WORLD
ECONOMY

I. WHAT IS THE WORLD ECONOMY?

IN MANY WAYS, we are all part of the world economy. When we drink our imported coffee in the morning, when we use a foreign-made CD player, or when we travel abroad on holiday, we are participating in the growing world of international trade and finance.

And it is not only as a consumer of foreign goods and services that we are part of the world economy. The money that our pension funds or university endowments earn from global investments may actually be paying for our retirement or a new building on campus. Foreign investment in local real estate and local companies can also provide needed jobs for our friends and families. Even the local athlete who has signed a contract to play abroad is part of the expanding global economy.

The world economy consists of all those interactions among people, businesses, and governments that cross international borders, even the illegal ones. If we buy drugs—or we join the fight against drugs by helping Latin American farmers substitute food crops for coca—we become part of the world economy. We also use the world economy to achieve specific political or ecological objectives when we employ economic sanctions to fight human rights abuses or to stop the illegal killing of endangered species in other countries.

Basically, whatever crosses an international border—whether goods, services, or transfers of funds—is part of the world economy. Food imports, automobile exports, global investments, even trade in services such as movies or tourism, contribute to each country's international economic activity.

2. HOW IS WEALTH DETERMINED AROUND
THE WORLD?

A NATION'S WEALTH CAN best be determined by looking at its people. But which statistic do we rely on? Are the Kuwaitis better off because they earn more money than the Brazilians? Are the French better off if they have more telephones per household than the Japanese? Are the Italians better off because they have more savings than Americans?

There are many different ways to determine wealth, and each country tends to look at a different group of statistics. Most economists define wealth as what a person owns, such as stocks and real estate, but most people look first to their level of income, or salary, to see if they are well off.

Comparing salaries in different countries, however, is like comparing apples and oranges, because salaries in each country are paid in different currencies. Is a French salary of 500,000 French francs worth more than a Canadian salary of 100,000 Canadian dollars? We need to somehow translate what each person earns into a common unit of measure.

One way of translating salaries is to first compare the value of each currency. This is usually done by using exchange rates, which tell us the value of one currency calculated in terms of another. Currency exchange rates, set by the foreign exchange markets around the world, reflect the markets' view of each country's economic and political system. Exchange rates can be used to convert a Tokyo resident's yen salary into dollars, allowing us to compare it to a U.S. dollar salary in Los Angeles.

But what can these salaries actually buy? Because the cost of living varies widely from one country to another, it is difficult to compare salaries by using currency exchange rates. If a Big Mac or a two-room apartment costs three times as much in Tokyo as in Los Angeles, a higher salary in Japan does not necessarily mean a Japanese worker is better off than an American.

It is therefore important to look at what salaries can really buy in each country. A salary's "purchasing power" tells us how many goods and services it can buy. Comparing the costs of a group of goods and services—a "basket" of products including housing, haircuts, food, movie tickets, and so forth—can give us a more reliable exchange rate, called *purchasing power parity* (*PPP*).

This "real" exchange rate, "PPP," then allows us to compare the purchasing power or "real" value of salaries from country to country. Although one country may be richer in terms of the amount of money each citizen owns or earns, calculated by traditional exchange rates, what counts in the long run is what each person can do with this wealth.

3. WHAT IS MACROECONOMICS?

MACROECONOMICS PROVIDES US with a bird's-eye view of a country's economic landscape. Instead of looking at the behavior of individual businesses and consumers—called *microeconomics*—the goal of macroeconomics is to look at overall economic trends such as employment levels, economic growth, balance of payments, and inflation. The study of the world economy is essentially a *macroeconomic* survey.

Just as the speed of an engine is regulated by its supply of fuel, macroeconomics is influenced by the supply of money in any given economy. This is influenced mainly by *monetary policy*, which controls a nation's money supply, and *fiscal policy*, which controls the government's revenue and spending. Control over an economy is essentially in the hands of each country's central bank and its government, because they control the money that provides the fuel to keep the economy running.

Monetary policy, the control of a nation's money supply, is managed by each country's central bank. Germany's Bundesbank, Britain's Bank of England, and the Bank of Japan all regulate their money supplies with the same basic goals as the U.S. Federal Reserve: to promote economic growth and keep inflation in check.

Just as a driver uses the accelerator to speed up or slow down a vehicle, central banks control the economy by increasing or decreasing the money supply. By carefully regulating the supply of money to fuel economic growth, a central bank works to keep the economy from overheating or from slowing down too quickly.

Monetary policy is essentially a guessing game. Despite the tendency of television or radio business news programs to concentrate on the latest government statistics, there is no one single indicator that tells us how fast an economy is growing. And there is no way to know how quickly the economy will respond to political or fiscal changes that may take months or years to implement. In general, central banks try to keep one eye on inflation, which is produced by an overheating economy, and one eye on unemployment, the result of an economic slowdown.

The economy can also be controlled by regulating fiscal policy—essentially government taxing and spending. Just as a family's economic health is influenced by the parents' earning and spending habits, a nation's economic health is influenced by the government's fiscal policies, such as taxation, spending, and government borrowing.

For better or for worse, the major economic influences in our daily lives, such as inflation and unemployment, are primarily the result of macroeconomic decisions.

4. HOW DOES INTERNATIONAL TRADE
FUNCTION?

WHEN THE SWISS export chocolate to Honduras, they can use the money they earn to import Honduran bananas—or they can use it to pay for Saudi Arabian oil or vacations in Hawaii. The basic idea of international trade and investment is simple: each country produces goods or services that can be either consumed at home or exported to other countries. The money earned from these exports can then be used to pay for imports of goods and services.

The main difference between domestic trade and international trade is the use of foreign currencies. Goods crossing international borders can be paid for in the local currency or any other internationally accepted currency.

Although global trade is often added up in U.S. dollars, the trading itself can involve a myriad of currencies. In Paris, an imported Japanese CD player is first purchased from a Tokyo exporter with yen, but then sold for French francs on the Champs Élysée. In Seattle, French designer sunglasses are sold for U.S. dollars, but purchased from the Paris exporter in French francs. Brazilian coffee, American films, and German automobiles are sold around the world in currencies as diverse as Danish kroner and Malaysian ringgits.

Whenever a country imports or exports goods and services, there is a resulting flow of funds: money returns to the exporting nation, and money flows out of the importing nation. Trade and investment is a two-way street. Money flowing to

Tokyo doesn't just sit around collecting dust. It is usually invested in other countries, or used to purchase other imported goods and services.

With a minimum of trade barriers, international trade and investment usually make everyone better off. In a truly interlinked global economy, consumers are given the opportunity to buy the best products at the best prices. By opening up markets, a government allows its citizens to export those things they are best at producing, and to import the rest, choosing from the best the world has to offer.

Some trade barriers will always exist as long as any two countries have different sets of laws. However, when a country decides to protect its economy by erecting artificial trade barriers, the result often damages everyone, including those people the barriers were originally meant to protect.

The Great Depression of the 1930s, for example, spread around the world when the United States decided to erect trade barriers to protect local producers. As other countries retaliated, trade plummeted, jobs were lost, and the world entered a long period of economic decline.

5. WHAT ARE TRADE SURPLUSES AND DEFICITS?

JUST LIKE ANY BUSINESS, a country has to keep track of its inflow and outflow of goods, services, and payments. At the end of any given period, each country has to look at its "bottom line" and add up its international trade and investments.

The narrowest measure of a country's trade, the *merchandise trade balance*, looks only at "visible" goods such as motorcycles, wine, and videocassette recorders. Trade in visible goods is often referred to in the press as the "trade balance" even though it includes only those tangible goods that can actually be loaded on a ship, airplane, or other means of transport used to move goods from one country to another.

But what about the trade in services such as Hollywood movies and Japanese video-game software? The *current account* gives a comprehensive picture of international trade because it includes a country's exports and imports of services, in addition to its visible trade. It may not be obvious, but many countries make a lot of money exporting "invisibles" such as banking, movies, and tourism. A tourist abroad, for example, "buys" hotel and restaurant services in the same way a consumer at home would buy an imported appliance.

By looking at its current account, we can tell which countries have been profitable traders—running a surplus, with money in the bank at the end of each year—and which countries have been unprofitable traders, spending more than they've earned. A country can't run a current account deficit for too long before it is forced to start spending money to support its currency on the international markets. The decline of the U.S. dollar in the mid-1990s, for example, was directly linked to the fact that the United States was consistently running huge trade deficits.

Trade deficits and surpluses have to be balanced by payments that make up the difference. A country with a current account surplus, for example, can use the extra money to invest abroad, or it can put it in its "cookie jar" of foreign currency reserves. On the other hand, a country running a current account deficit has to look abroad for loans or investments, or maybe even dip into its own reserves to pay for its excessive imports. All these payments and transfers of funds are included in a country's *capital account*.

The widest measure of a country's trade is called its *balance of payments*. It includes not only payments abroad, but all of the goods, services, and transfers of funds that cross international borders. The balance of payments adds up everything in a country's current account and capital account. Since all of a country's trade in goods and services is "balanced" by the international transfers of funds, the balance of payments should add up to zero at the end of the accounting period. Every banana, every automobile, every investment, and every payment that crosses a country's borders is included in the final tally of international trade and investment—the balance of payments.

6. HOW DOES FOREIGN OWNERSHIP AFFECT A COUNTRY'S ECONOMY?

IT IS OFTEN SAID that the only thing worse than being talked about is *not* being talked about. Countries with open economies could likewise complain that the only thing worse than foreign investment is *no* foreign investment.

When Americans criticize the Japanese for "buying up America," with large parcels of U.S. real estate in Japanese hands, or when the French criticize the Americans for "buying up France," with many French companies and even Euro Disneyland under American control, they choose to ignore one of the basic components of international trade: the need to invest abroad.

Basically, foreign investments are the result of trade surpluses. When a hardworking country exports more than it imports, it ends up with money to invest in the global economy. This money can be used abroad to buy anything from foreign government bonds to real estate and whole companies. The United States, for example, has a long history of investing in other countries whenever it runs trade surpluses. However, when the United States began running trade deficits in the 1980s, the billions of dollars spent by Americans on foreign goods returned as foreign investments in the U.S. economy. Despite the criticism these investments received, they did help to keep the American economy running on track and created many new jobs for local workers.

Because there is a natural fear of strategic industries

falling into foreign hands, most countries—including the United States—have laws that prohibit foreign ownership of vital high-tech industries and military suppliers. This is usually accomplished without limiting foreign investment in other sectors of the economy.

Countries with trade deficits can often benefit from foreign challenges to make their industries more competitive on the international markets. By the mid-1990s, U.S. car makers had succeeded in increasing their sales abroad, mainly because Japanese competition in the U.S. market forced them to make higher-quality automobiles at competitive prices. In the long run, competition forces everyone to do a better job. If a country chooses to restrict foreign investment, jobs and needed capital are often lost to other countries with more open economies.

7. WHAT IS MONEY?

CONTRARY TO POPULAR belief, money does not really make the world go around: the global economy runs on the trade of goods and services. But without money, trade would be a very difficult undertaking indeed.

Imagine trying to send strawberries to France and waiting to be paid with the next shipment of cheese. Or imagine having too many strawberries one year and trying to save them to ship later. And how many strawberries is a piece of cheese worth anyway?

These issues can be resolved by using something that represents value. Let's call it money. A mark, a yen, a buck, or a pound—the name is not important. These pieces of metal and paper serve to facilitate trade in three ways: they serve as a medium of exchange, allowing strawberries to be sold for money instead of cheese; they allow value to be stored from one year to the next—unlike strawberries, currencies don't rot; and they serve as a unit of account, telling us how much strawberries are worth in something that is universally understood.

The earliest money, shells and beads, served the same role that paper, credit cards, and electronic transfers serve today. Money makes trade more manageable. When a product is sold for money, this money can then be used to buy other products. By serving as a medium of exchange, money acts as a go-between for all transactions of goods and services that make up the world economy.

By using money to store value, a producer can avoid a warehouse full of rotting goods. After selling a product for money, a producer can sit back and wait for the best time to purchase other goods and services. During this time, the money can be put under a mattress or it can be invested to earn interest. This allows the stored money to keep pace with inflation—or even outpace it.

Finally, by using money as a unit of account, goods and services can be evaluated by using a common measure. Money not only tells us how many strawberries a piece of cheese is worth, but how many apples it takes to buy an airline ticket or how many hamburgers it takes to buy a haircut. Money allows for all goods and services to be expressed in terms of a standardized unit, and worldwide trade is made immeasurably easier.

MAJOR CURRENCIES AROUND THE WORLD

COUNTRY	CURRENCY	VALUE (IN UNITS PER U.S. DOLLAR)		
		1985	1990	1995
Africa				
Kenya	shilling	14.7	24.0	44.9
Morocco	dirham	9.6	8.0	8.9
Senegal	CFA franc	378.0	254.4	534.1
South Africa	rand	2.6	3.4	3.5
The Americas				
Argentina	peso	0.8*	5,583	1.0*
Brazil	real	10,400	170.0*	0.8*
Canada	dollar	1.4	1.2	1.4
Mexico	peso	457.5	2,941	5.07*
United States	dollar	1.0	1.0	1.0
Asia/Pacific				
Australia	dollar	1.5	1.3	1.3
China	yuan (renminbi)	2.8	4.7	8.4
Hong Kong	dollar	7.8	7.8	7.7
India	rupee	12.1	17.8	31.4
Japan	yen	201.0	135.6	100.0
New Zealand	dollar	2.0	1.7	1.6
Europe				
Austria	schilling	17.3	10.5	10.9
Belgium	franc	50.4	31.0	31.8
Britain	pound	0.7	0.5	0.6
Denmark	krone	9.0	5.8	6.1
European Community	ECU	1.1	0.7	0.82
Finland	markka	5.4	3.6	4.7
France	franc	7.6	5.1	5.4
Germany	mark	2.5	1.5	1.6
Greece	drachma	148.2	156.3	241.5
Italy	lira	1,683	1,128	1,621
Netherlands	guilder	2.8	1.7	1.7
Norway	krone	7.6	5.9	6.8
Portugal	escudo	158.7	132.3	159.8

Country	Currency	Value (in units per U.S. dollar)		
		1985	1990	1995
Europe (cont.)				
Spain	peseta	154.5	95.2	132.4
Sweden	krona	7.6	5.6	7.4
Switzerland	franc	2.1	1.3	1.3
Middle East				
Egypt	pound	1.3	2.9	3.4
Iraq	dinar	0.3	0.3	0.6
Israel	shekel	1,484	2.1*	1,729
Saudi Arabia	riyal	3.6	3.7	3.7
Turkey	lira	579.1	2,874	40,390

*Readjusted in a currency revaluation program.

8. WHAT ARE THE WORLD'S MAJOR CURRENCIES?

THE CURRENCIES OF the world's major economies have names—and backgrounds—that are as diverse as the countries themselves.

The name *dollar*, used in many countries, including the United States, Canada, and Australia, comes from a silver coin minted during the Middle Ages in a small valley, or "Thal," in Bohemia called Joachimsthal. Just as a sausage from Frankfurt came to be called a frankfurter, the coins from Joachimsthal were called "Joachimsthaler" or simply "Thaler," and came to be called "dollar" in English.

The *pound*, used in Britain, Egypt, and Lebanon, among other countries, refers to the weights used in minting the currency, originally one Roman pound (12 ounces) of silver. The word *penny* has the same origin as the word *pawn*, found in terms such as *pawn shop*, and originally meant "to pledge." A penny, like any currency, is a "pledge" of value.

In Italy and Turkey, the currency is called the *lira*. The word is based on the Latin *libra*, meaning "pound," and refers to the weight of the original coins.

In Spanish, the word meaning "weight," *peso*, is used to describe the coins that were based on a certain weight of gold or silver. Originally, there were gold coins called *peso de oro* and silver ones called *peso de plata*. In Spain, the currency is called *peseta*, meaning "small peso." The word *peso* is used to describe the currency in many Spanish-speaking countries of Latin America.

In Denmark, Norway, and Sweden, the word for crown—*krone* in Denmark and Norway, *krona* in Sweden—is used to describe the currency that was originally minted by the king or queen, with royal crowns stamped on the original coins. Today, the crown has been replaced by other symbols, but the name remains.

The *franc*, used in France, Switzerland, Belgium, and other countries and territories, is based on the early coins used in France that bore the Latin inscription *franconium rex*, meaning "king of the Franks." The coin, as well as the country of France, took its name from one of the tribes that originally settled in the area, the Franks.

The German *mark* and Finnish *markka* derive their names from the small marks that were cut into coins to indicate their precious metal content. The German mark, or *deutsche mark*, is often called by its shortened name, the D-mark.

The *riyal*, in Saudi Arabia and Qatar, and the *rial* in Iran, are based on the Spanish word *real*—which was derived from the Latin *regal(is)*, referring to earlier "royal" coins.

The *dinar*, used in Iraq and Kuwait, among other countries, derives its name from *denarius*, a Roman coin.

In India, Pakistan, and other neighboring countries of the subcontinent, the currency is called *rupee* (in Indonesia, *rupiah*), based on the Sanskrit word *rupya*, meaning "coined silver."

The ancient Chinese word *yiam* meant "round," or "small round thing." The name of the Japanese currency, the *yen*, and the name of the Chinese currency, the *yuan*, both derived from the old Chinese word *yiam*, refer to the round shape of the original coins.

9. WHAT ARE FREELY FLOATING CURRENCIES?

APART FROM A few misguided misers like Ebenezer Scrooge, no one wants a currency "to have and to hold, until death do you part." Currencies are used to buy goods and services, both at home and abroad, and their value is determined in many different ways.

It used to be that a currency's value was fixed by its government or was linked to some item of value. In the United States, for example, until 1971, dollars held by foreigners could be converted into gold. This *gold standard* was meant to guarantee that currencies would always have a fixed value, determined by the amount of gold in each country's vaults. This is no longer the case.

Most countries had already abandoned the gold standard in the 1930s, when insufficient gold reserves forced governments to adopt a system of fixed exchange rates, where each country's government decided, on its own, what its currency was worth. The British government, for example, could decide that it would only allow pounds to be exchanged for U.S. dollars at a rate of $2.40 per British pound.

This artificial system of fixed rates gave way to a free market of currency values when the Smithsonian Agreement of fixed exchange rates collapsed in 1973. The world's major currencies were then allowed to "float" freely on the international markets.

The British pound may now be worth $2.00 one month and $1.50 the next, depending on what the world's foreign exchange markets determine. Just like a concert ticket on the night of a sold-out performance, a freely floating currency's price goes up when there is increased demand.

It is hard to envision, but currencies are "scarce" commodities, like apples and crude oil. Their price depends on available supply—how much has been printed by governments or central banks—and on the demand for any particular currency in the marketplace. When everyone wants to buy Japanese stereo systems, for example, the "price" of the yen tends to go up. This happens because importers in Paris and Seattle have to use their francs and dollars to "buy" yen to pay for Japanese products.

Likewise, if Italians should all decide to go on vacation in Florida, the Italian lira will lose value as it is sold on the foreign exchange markets to buy dollars that are then used to pay for Mickey Mouse T-shirts and Disney World admission tickets. All of the world's major currencies—such as the U.S. dollar, the Swiss franc, and the Japanese yen—are allowed to fluctuate freely on the world's foreign exchange, or *forex*, markets.

This "free-float" system does not keep governments from trying to influence the value of their currency by buying or selling on the open markets. When the British government wants the value of the pound to go up, it merely goes out and buys several billion dollars worth of British pounds on the markets, driving up the price. The present system, sometimes called a "dirty float," allows periodic central bank intervention to regulate the value of currencies to keep them from rising or falling too rapidly. Some currencies, such as those in the European Monetary System, are not allowed to rise or fall outside a predetermined range.

However, like trying to reverse the flow of water, it is very difficult to halt the slide of a currency if the traders and investors decide it is headed for a fall. In the early 1990s, currencies such as the British pound and Italian lira were forced to withdraw from the European Monetary System after their governments spent untold trillions to support them. In the end, the currencies fell in value, and those who had "bet" on their decline, including some private investors, were able to reap enormous profits from their speculative activities.

Because of the enormous amount of currencies traded every day on the foreign exchange markets, interventions by the central banks usually only succeed in slowing a currency's inevitable rise or fall.

10. WHAT ARE EXCHANGE RATES?

IF EVERY COUNTRY in the world used the same currency, international trade would be made much easier. Unfortunately, this is not the case: a Copenhagen beer producer wants to be paid in Danish kroner, and a Hong Kong shirt maker wants to be paid in Hong Kong dollars.

What is a currency worth? Currencies, like other commodities, such as beer and shirts, have a certain value. The only difference is that each currency's value is stated in terms of other currencies. French francs have a value in U.S. dollars, which have a value in British pounds, which have a value in Japanese yen. These *exchange rates* change constantly, depending on the market for them, and are updated constantly in banks and foreign exchange offices around the world.

These "forex" markets keep track of the values of all of the world's major currencies. As some increase in value, others decline. When a French franc goes up in value against the U.S. dollar, the dollar must go down in value against the French franc. At the same time, the French franc may decline in value against the British pound, meaning that the dollar declines even more in terms of the pound. Foreign exchange is a constantly changing twenty-four-hours-a-day market, with trading in hundreds of financial centers around the world, from Singapore to San Francisco and from London to Buenos Aires.

These markets are all linked electronically. Banks and "Bureaus de Change" look at this global interbank market to set their daily rates. When we change money while on vacation—whether we are in Florence, Tahiti, or Acapulco—the exchange rate is determined by the global market.

Anyone traveling abroad will notice that the exchange rate is slightly different if the customer is buying or selling any one particular currency. This "spread" between the buy and sell rates ensures that the banks and exchange bureaus make a small profit on every transaction. This means that an indecisive traveler, by exchanging money back and forth several times, would end up with a lot less money, after losing a few percentage points in spreads and commissions on each foreign exchange transaction.

How do the foreign exchange markets decide how much a currency is worth? The prices of freely floating currencies are influenced by economic and political events and sometimes by the speculation of individual traders. Foreign exchange traders, like traders in grain or pork bellies, sometimes "bet" that a currency will increase in value. If interest rates fall in Tokyo, traders may rush to sell yen and buy dollars, hoping to get a higher return on their investments. If the Swedish economy looks strong, the krona may increase in value; but if it looks as though inflation is returning, the krona may decline against currencies with lower inflation.

Likewise, during periods of economic and political turmoil, the world's traders and investors often turn to a particular currency as a refuge. When political or social unrest threatens currencies around the world, traders and investors often rush to buy "hard" currencies such as the Swiss franc and the U.S. dollar, which are expected to preserve their value in times of trouble.

11. WHAT IS GNP?

IN EVERY COUNTRY—from the Philippines to Poland and from Cuba to Kuwait—the production of goods and services provides what it takes for people to survive and prosper.

Some countries produce an abundance of raw materials, such as coal and timber, while others produce an abundance of manufactured goods, such as televisions and automobiles. Some countries may concentrate on producing goods, such as washing machines, while others produce services, such as movies, insurance, or banking. Whatever is not consumed in the country itself can be sold to other countries as exports.

The size of a country's economy is determined by the total amount of goods and services that it produces. As more goods and services are produced, the economy grows—and the best way to measure this growth is to put a monetary value on everything bought or sold.

Although money is not the only way to measure an economy's size, it is the easiest way to sum up the value of all the apples and oranges, football games and computers, automobiles and college classes that a country produces in the course of a given year.

The monetary value of all these goods and services can then be added up and compared with that of other countries. Since almost every country uses a different currency, the totals from each country have to be translated—by using currency exchange rates—to compare the size of one country's economy to another. For example, the yen value of the Japanese economy can be converted into U.S. dollars to compare it to the American economy.

The measure of economic activity that includes all the goods and services bought or sold in a country over the course of a year is called *gross domestic product* (*GDP*). Just as a speedometer is used to measure the speed of a car, GDP measures a country's total economic activity. When a country produces more goods and services, its economic activity speeds up. In other words, GDP increases. A healthy economy tends to grow steadily, over a long period. When growth stops or slows, the economy is said to be in a "recession."

What happens to the goods and services sold abroad? When the international activities of a country's residents are added to GDP, a wider, more global measure of a country's total economic activity is created: *gross national product* (*GNP*).

Both measures tell more or less the same story—GDP concentrates on the purely "domestic" production of goods and services, covering only the economic activity that takes place within the country's borders, while GNP includes net international trade and investment, which includes everything from exports of toys and aircraft to foreign earnings and money spent on travel abroad.

GDP and GNP try to measure every legal good and service that an economy produces. A farmer selling fresh vegetables, an automobile dealer selling used cars, a poet selling a new book, a hairdresser, prize fighter, or lifeguard selling their goods and services—all contribute to economic activity, as measured by GDP and GNP. At each stage of production, every time monetary value is added, a country's GDP and GNP are increased.

12. WHAT IS INFLATION?

IT USED TO be that reports of a strong economy brought euphoria to the world markets. When factories were producing at full capacity and the number of unemployed people declined, the markets would greet the news with approval, confident that in a booming economy everyone would be better off.

However, after the severe inflation scares of the past decades, with prices rising out of control, governments and markets realized that an economy that grows too quickly could be a bad thing. With a sharp drop in unemployment, companies are forced to pay higher wages for scarce workers, and prices of goods and services are raised to pay for their increased costs. Inflation has now become one of the world economy's greatest fears. Inflation tends to be highest during times of economic turmoil, such as energy shocks, wars, or debt crises.

Each country keeps track of inflation by looking at the prices of a group or "basket" of consumer goods and services. This is called the *consumer price index* (*CPI*) in the United States and the *retail price index* (*RPI*) in Britain. *Inflation* is usually defined as the percentage rise in the costs of that basket of goods and services over a given period. *Deflation*, a decline in these prices, rarely occurs because companies and employees are reluctant to allow their prices and salaries to be reduced.

In a booming economy, inflation begins to rise as consumers and businesses compete with each other for goods and services, bidding up prices in their frenzy to buy a limited quantity of products. The increase in prices usually leads workers to ask for increasingly higher wages to "keep up with inflation." The result is often a vicious circle of wage and price increases that end up hurting almost everyone, especially those on fixed incomes, who see their buying power decline when their incomes are not adjusted for the rise in prices.

Normally, when governments and central banks see signs of inflation, they try to slow down the economy. They slam on the brakes by increasing interest rates, which makes almost all activities, such as buying new cars or building new factories, more expensive. Higher interest rates usually discourage business and consumer spending, leading to a reduction in jobs and a slowdown in the economy.

The international markets watch each country's inflation rate very carefully, always looking for signs of stable economic growth and low inflation rates. International investors, such as pension funds and banks, move billions and sometimes trillions of dollars, marks, and yen around the world on any given day, looking for the best return on their investment.

With favorable inflation and interest rates, a country attracts foreign investment and the money comes flooding in. When a country's economy grows too strongly, however, and it looks as if runaway inflation is about to rear its ugly head, international investors quickly move their money out, preferring to invest their funds in countries with more stable economic growth and predictable inflation rates.

13. HOW CAN THE WORLD'S ECONOMIES BE COMPARED?

IF A SMALL country like Ireland or Sri Lanka were to win all of the gold medals at the Summer Olympics, it would mean a lot more than a victory by a large country like China or the United States. In the same way, it would be difficult to evaluate the economic achievements of any country without looking at its size and the resources at its disposal.

For example, what does it mean to say that the United States spends more money on its military than Switzerland? If Switzerland is only a fraction of the size of the United States, comparing gross figures between the two countries is rarely useful.

To compare countries in the world economy, economic statistics have to be related to the countries' size and translated into a commonly accepted unit of measure. U.S. military spending, for example, can be compared to the military spending of Switzerland by relating it to the size of its total economy, measured either by

GDP (gross domestic product) or GNP (gross national product). It would then become meaningful to say that U.S. military spending was only 8 percent of its GDP during a given period, while it was more than 10 percent in Switzerland during the same period.

Comparing a country's earnings or spending to its GDP or its GNP is a valuable way of comparing economies. Neither GDP nor GNP, however, completely measures the size of a country's total economy. Illegal activities, such as drug sales or prostitution, are never reported and are consequently not included in these "official" measures. In addition, work done for no salary, such as housework or volunteer work at hospitals and schools, is not included, since no payment is made for these goods and services. A country with a high level of working parents would consequently show a larger GDP, reflecting the added costs of day care and cleaning services otherwise provided "for free" by a stay-at-home spouse.

Although neither GDP nor GNP is a perfect measure of the size of a country's economy, they still provide the best means we have for comparing the economic activity of different countries, big and small, rich and poor.

14. WHAT IS MONEY SUPPLY?

EVERY ECONOMY IN the world is controlled by its supply of money. Even an "economy" as small as a Monopoly game is controlled by the supply of "Monopoly money" used to buy and sell houses and property around the board.

All modern economies are based on the use of money.

Each country's money supply, therefore, determines how quickly the economy can grow. If the central bank increases the money supply, consumers and businesses have more money to spend on goods and services.

Just as the game of Monopoly can be stimulated by increasing the amount of money available to its players, a country can encourage economic growth by increasing its money supply, which includes currency in circulation and readily available funds such as bank deposits on which checks can be drawn. This "narrow" measure is usually called "M1" because it refers to the first level of money supply. This easy-to-access money, often called "high-powered" money, tends to fuel most consumer and business consumption and therefore stimulates most economic growth. Other measures of a country's money supply include funds that are not so readily available, such as time deposits and other long-term investments.

Basically, when businesses and individuals have less money at their disposal, economic activity slows. Central banks usually limit money supply growth in order to slow down the economy and control inflation. In a Monopoly game, with less money floating around the board, for example, players will pay less money when buying properties from other players.

On the larger scale of a national economy, less money usually leads to an economic slowdown. When less money is available, interest rates tend to increase—the cost of money increases—and it becomes more expensive to borrow. If it costs more to borrow money, businesses and consumers will be less inclined to increase spending. In this way, control of the money supply allows a central bank to reduce inflation.

The money supply can also be increased to stimulate economic activity. If the players in a Monopoly game are given more than two hundred dollars for passing Go—five hundred dollars, say—the results are predictable: the "economy" speeds up and players start buying and selling at higher and higher prices. Increasing the money supply usually results in rapid growth and inflated prices.

15. WHAT IS A CENTRAL BANK?

JUST AS A PRUDENT driver keeps an eye on the road and a steady hand on the wheel, every country uses a central bank to keep the nation's economy on course. Central banks monitor economic data and adjust the money supply and interest rates in an effort to keep the economy headed in the right direction.

Instead of taking deposits and making loans like normal banks, a central bank—such as the U.S. Federal Reserve or the Bank of Japan—controls the economy by increasing or decreasing the country's supply of money. Cranking up the printing presses is not the only way for a central bank to increase the economy's supply of money.

In fact, in most modern economies printed notes and coins are only a small percentage—often less than 10 percent—of the total money supply. Central banks usually print only enough currency to satisfy the everyday needs of business and consumers. The U.S. Federal Reserve, for example, has the Bureau of Printing and Engraving print up bills from time to time to replace worn-out money in the economy at large.

A central bank is actually much more than a national piggy bank, providing the money for each country's economy.

Besides coordinating the country's monetary policy, it serves as a watchdog to supervise the banking system, in most cases acting independently of its government to provide a stabilizing influence on the country's economy.

The activities and responsibilities of central banks vary widely from country to country. Britain's Bank of England, for example, is responsible for printing the money as well as supervising the banking system and coordinating monetary policy. In the United States, the duties of a central bank are divided among different agencies: the U.S. Treasury borrows money for the government's use through Treasury bond and note issues, while the Federal Reserve Board is in charge of monetary policy and oversees the printing at the Bureau of Printing and Engraving.

The French central bank, the Banque de France, prints and issues the country's money, but the French treasury makes the major decisions regarding monetary policy and bank supervision. Germany's central bank, called the Bundesbank—*Bund* means "federal"—is noted for its active policy of strict monetary control. This policy consists of limiting money supply growth in order to control inflation at all costs. The Bundesbank's reputation for responsible monetary policy has led the European Union to base its central banking operations in Frankfurt.

The Bank of Japan, like many of the world's central banks, acts as banker to the government. This activity is a major source of revenue for the bank, since fees are charged for issuing the government's checks and for holding its deposits of foreign currencies. Some central banks, such as the Swiss National Bank, are at least partly owned by private shareholders.

During times of financial panic, central banks also act as a "lender of last resort," providing funds to shore up failing banks in order to preserve the stability of the financial system.

In times of international crisis, central banks sometimes

turn to their own central authority, the Bank for International Settlements (BIS), which is based in Basel, Switzerland. In addition to advising and supervising of the international banking community, the BIS can provide temporary funds to shore up failing banking systems. The BIS often provides short-term financing called *bridge loans*, which are paid back as soon as longer-term financing can be arranged.

Central banks also use the Bank for International Settlements to transfer funds to other central banks around the world. The French government, for example, may use the BIS to facilitate a payment to Nigeria's central bank—or the Bank of Japan may use the BIS to transfer funds to the U.S. Federal Reserve. The key for any international transfer is to have a central clearing authority that credits the accounts of the bank receiving the money and debits the account of the other bank. No actual money ever changes hands—it doesn't have to, as long as a central bank keeps track of the payments.

In fact, international payments through central banks are handled in the same way as checks are cashed at a neighborhood bank. One client's account is credited and the account writing the check is simply debited. This system of crediting one account and debiting another makes it possible to settle international payments without having to actually deliver the money. In a way, the Bank for International Settlements acts as a central bank to the world's central banks.

16. HOW DO CENTRAL BANKS REGULATE AN
ECONOMY?

DESPITE THE PRACTICE of Donald Duck's miserly
Uncle Scrooge, most savings in an economy are not stored
as notes or coins in a home vault, but in the form of bank deposits.

Since most money in an economy is actually nothing more
than a savings or checking account at a local bank, the most effective way for a central bank to control the economy is to increase or decrease bank lending and bank deposits. When banks
have money to lend to their customers, the economy grows.
When the banks are forced to cut back lending, the economy
slows.

Once a customer deposits money in a local bank, it becomes available for further lending. A hundred dollars deposited
in a bank in San Francisco, for example, doesn't lie idle for long.
After setting aside a small amount of each deposit as a "reserve,"
the bank can lend out the remainder, further increasing the
money supply—without any new currency being printed. When
these loans are redeposited in banks, more money becomes
available for new loans, increasing the money supply even more.
A bank's supply of money for lending is limited only by its deposits and its *reserve requirements*, which are determined by the
central bank.

This "reserve requirement" has become one of the most
effective tools used by central banks to control the money supply. When a bank is required to keep a certain percentage of its

funds on reserve with the central bank—10 percent of deposits, for example—it is unable to lend these funds back to customers.

When a central bank decides to increase the money supply, it can reduce this reserve requirement, allowing banks to use more of their funds to lend to businesses and consumers. This increases the money supply quickly because of a multiplier effect: as the new loans enter the economy, deposits increase—and banks have even more money to lend. This, in turn, generates further deposits, providing more money for further loans.

Another way of controlling the money supply is to raise or lower interest rates. When a central bank decides that the economy is growing too slowly—or not growing at all—it can reduce the interest rate it charges on its loans to the country's banks. If banks are allowed to get cheaper money at the central bank, they can make cheaper loans to businesses and consumers, providing an important stimulus to economic growth. Alternatively, if the economy shows signs of growing too quickly, a central bank can increase the interest rate on its loans to banks, putting the brakes on economic growth.

Perhaps the most dramatic way of increasing or decreasing the money supply is through *open market operations*, where a central bank buys or sells large amounts of securities, such as government treasury bonds, in the open market. By buying a large block of bonds, from a bank or a securities house for example, the central bank pumps money into the economy because it uses funds that previously were not part of the money supply. The money used to buy bonds in open market operations then becomes available for banks to lend out to consumers and businesses.

In a sense, the central bank creates money every time it dips into its vaults to buy bonds in the open market. Whether it uses a check, pays cash, or simply credits the bank's account at the central bank, the funds for an open market purchase enter the money supply for the first time. A central bank, unlike other players in the economy, does not have to secure funding from any other source. It can simply print more money or use its nearly unlimited credit with banks in the system. This "black hole" of central bank funds is virtually an enclosed system, separate from the economy's money supply as a whole.

Once a central bank's payment enters the economy, it becomes part of the money supply, providing fuel for businesses and consumers to increase their economic activities. Likewise, when a central bank sells bonds in the open market, it reduces the money supply. The payments from banks and securities houses for the bonds sold by the central bank disappear into the central bank's "vaults," completely removed from the economy at large.

An error in judgment at the central bank can have grave consequences for everyone in the economy. If a central bank allows the economy to expand too rapidly by keeping too much money in circulation, it may cause inflation. If it slows down the economy by removing too much money from circulation, an economic recession could result, bringing unwanted unemployment and reduced production.

17. HOW ARE INTEREST RATES USED TO CONTROL AN ECONOMY?

IN FREE-MARKET economies, consumers and businesses can do almost anything they want as long as they pay for it. Therefore, by controlling interest rates—the cost of money— central banks are able to influence economic growth.

In a totalitarian country the government can simply tell its citizens what it wants them to do. But in free market countries, consumers and businesses are encouraged to increase or reduce their economic activity through a variety of economic incentives. By increasing short-term interest rates, for example, a central bank discourages bank lending, reducing the amount of money available for business expansion and consumer spending. Likewise, by lowering these interest rates, a central bank acts to encourage economic activity.

Banks often borrow money from the central bank to lend to consumers and businesses. When a central bank decides to change its *discount rate*, the interest rate it charges for loans to banks, interest rates across the nation almost always follow suit. The interest rates on loans made between banks—called *interbank rates* in Europe and *Fed Funds rates* in the United States— tend to rise whenever banks have to pay more to borrow money themselves.

All interest rates are linked, because money, like most commodities, is interchangeable. Banks and individuals will go wherever interest rates are lowest—basically, wherever money is cheapest—so a change in interest rates announced in Washington will affect interest rates in Singapore.

In the global village of the international money markets, interest rates have become the heartbeat of economic activity, regulating economic growth worldwide. A country's consumers and businesses, therefore, can be directly affected by central bank decisions made on the other side of the world. Foreign investment money can come flooding in at a moment's notice, or be pulled out just as quickly if one country's interest rates are not kept in line with other countries in the world economy.

18. WHAT IS FREE TRADE?

WHEN EVERY COUNTRY is allowed to do what it does best—letting the French excel in fashion, the Japanese in electronics, and the Americans in aircraft, for example—the world economy prospers. With free trade, whoever produces the best product at the best price can sell that product around the world, benefiting consumers everywhere.

By encouraging free trade, countries expose their own producers to foreign competition, which can be disastrous for many poorly managed companies. This can lead to short-term layoffs and idle factories. In the long run, however, foreign competition usually forces companies to be more efficient and more competitive, helping the country to become a successful and profitable member of the global economy.

Free trade is based on the notion of open markets. With a level playing field, companies in one country can compete equitably with companies in other countries to sell their goods and services.

The best way for a government to encourage a new trading partner is to remove restrictions and barriers to its internal market. This courtesy, called "most favored nation" status in the United States, is provided to countries whose political and economic policies are seen to merit favored treatment.

Countries may also encourage trade by allowing importers and exporters to barter goods. In some Eastern European countries, for example, bartering may involve trading a shipment of Pepsi-Cola for a shipment of vodka, in order to overcome a temporary scarcity of hard currencies.

When a country wants to encourage its exports, it can provide incentives to make its products more competitive on the world market. Some countries provide loans or grants to foreign buyers of a country's goods and services through export-import banks. These state-supported "ex-im" banks provide low cost loans, called *export credits*, that stimulate exports. These loans are sometimes criticized for going too far, encouraging exports at the expense of otherwise competitive producers in other countries.

At times, countries might actually want to encourage imports of foreign goods and services, primarily to decrease international tensions resulting from trade balances. When Japan was criticized by Europe and the United States for running large trade surpluses, for example, the Japanese government undertook measures called "external adjustment." One of the most effective tools to stimulate imports is to increase the value of the country's currency, making foreign goods and services less expensive than locally made products.

A country may also encourage imports by stimulating its economy through lower interest rates, thus increasing purchases of foreign goods such as televisions and automobiles. In countries such as Germany, where many consumer goods are imported, lowering the interest rates can encourage imports of everything from Vietnamese rice to Canadian sporting goods.

Another way to encourage imports is to reduce cultural barriers that may limit purchases of foreign products. The Japanese government, for example, has tried to encourage Japanese consumers to buy more foreign products, such as U.S. beef or German automobiles, in an effort to ease the threat of re- taliatory trade sanctions from its uneasy trading partners.

19. WHAT ARE QUOTAS, TARIFFS, AND SUBSIDIES?

LIKE MOST WARS, a trade war can bring unwanted suf- fering, sometimes to those whom the war was originally meant to help. An inefficient car maker, for example, may ask for limits on foreign imports, hoping to keep its prices high without improving the quality of its product. In the end, how- ever, other countries may retaliate with trade restrictions of their own, limiting the access of the car maker to foreign markets.

By attempting to protect a few jobs in inefficient indus- tries, trade restrictions force consumers and businesses to buy poorly made and relatively expensive domestic products. In the end, the whole economy suffers by becoming less competitive on the international markets. The most common tools for limit- ing imports of foreign goods and services are quotas, tariffs, and subsidies.

When a country imposes a *quota*, it limits the quantity of certain foreign products that can be imported. A *tariff* is a tax placed on goods entering a country, raising the price of imported goods. A government can also use the taxpayers' money to provide a *subsidy* to local producers, making the price of local goods artificially lower than imported goods.

Trade barriers, like walls between feuding neighbors, are usually imposed unilaterally by one country acting on its own to limit imports. These barriers are designed to temporarily protect local producers from foreign competition and allow them time to improve productivity. The problem is that local producers rarely make the sacrifices to improve their products or lower their prices as long as they are protected from foreign competition by trade barriers.

Although trade restrictions are of dubious economic value, they have been shown to be effective in bringing about political or social change. The refusal of countries to trade and do business with South Africa, for example, was widely seen to be responsible for the decision to dismantle the system of apartheid. Similarly, closing the international markets to Haiti was an important factor in the fall of the military government, and eventually resulted in the return to democracy.

Trade blockades can be useful in forcing countries to change policies that violate human rights or international treaties, but only as long as a sufficient number of countries join in the blockade to make it effective.

20. HOW DO BUDGET DEFICITS AFFECT TRADE DEFICITS?

BUDGET DEFICITS AND trade deficits, while completely different events, often end up affecting each other—sometimes disastrously—for spendthrift economies.

The international shopping spree of American consumers and businesses during the 1980s was based on a surge in the dollar's value on the international markets. Swedish cars and French mineral water became much cheaper than similar U.S. products. Imports outpaced exports, sometimes to the tune of $100 billion per year—more than the size of many countries' total economy. These severe trade imbalances were caused, in part, by the persistent U.S. budget deficits.

A government's *budget deficit* is the amount by which government expenditures exceed tax revenues, while a *trade deficit* results from a country importing more than it exports. When faced with a budget deficit, most governments respond by issuing government bonds. Although these securities need to be paid back eventually, most governments find that it is political suicide to ask voters to pay higher taxes. They prefer to issue more government bonds to pay their bills. When it comes time to pay the interest on their bonds, governments usually issue even more bonds, going further into debt. If these borrowings are too large, however, it can have serious repercussions for the whole economy.

By borrowing to finance its budget deficits, a government pushes up interest rates. These higher interest rates attract foreign money looking for higher returns, increasing the value of the country's currency on the international markets. Imported goods then become as inexpensive as domestic substitutes. When imports become less expensive and exports harder to sell on the world markets, countries usually begin to run trade deficits.

The large U.S. trade deficits of the early 1990s, for example, were part of a vicious circle of budget deficits leading to record trade deficits that gave Japan and many other countries the dollars to spend on U.S. government bonds. In a way, the Japanese ended up trading videocassette recorders for pieces of paper—Treasury bonds that would one day have to be paid back by the U.S. government.

The awkward situation of one country using its trade surplus to pay for another government's budget deficits cannot last forever. Foreign investors eventually lose confidence in a country with chronic budget and trade deficits, and the time comes to pay the piper—the spendthrift country has to begin to pay back its debts. The result can sometimes be a collapsing currency and economic decline. Inevitably, every country has to decide to limit spending and bring its budget and trade deficits under control.

COMPANIES AROUND THE WORLD

COUNTRIES	TYPE OF COMPANY (IF APPLICABLE)	ABBR.	DEFINITION
United States		Inc.	Incorporated
England, Canada	Public	Plc	Public Limited Company
	Private	Ltd.	Limited
France, Belgium	Public	S.A.	Société Anonyme
	Private	Sarl	Société à responsabilité limitée
Spain, Mexico, etc.		S.A.	Sociedad Anónima
Brazil, Portugal, etc.		S.A.	Sociedade Anónima
Japan		Ltd.	Limited
Germany	Public	A.G.	Aktiengesellschaft
	Private	GmbH	Gesellschaft mit beschränkte Haftung
Netherlands	Public	N.V.	Naamloze Vennootschap
	Private	B.V.	Besloten Vennootschap
Italy	Public	SpA	Società per Azioni
	Private	Srl	Società a responsabilità limitata
Denmark		A/S	Aktieselskab

21. WHY ARE COMPANIES REFERRED TO AS LTD., INC., GMBH, OR S.A.?

THE HEART OF capitalism is private ownership, and a limited liability company allows people to own almost anything—from skyscrapers to television stations—without risking their personal assets should the company go bankrupt.

When an entrepreneur like Henry Ford begins a new company it is not a big problem to retain total responsibility and liability. However, once an enterprise starts to grow, a new structure, such as a partnership or a "company," would be required—the Ford Motor Company, for example. There are too many risks involved in a large enterprise, and no one wants to see their personal savings wiped out if a company goes bankrupt.

The key factor in owning any company is the guarantee—called *limited liability*—that assures that the owners of a company will never have to pay more than they have invested in the company. Their liabilities are limited in that when a company goes bankrupt, the owners can never be required to pay its unpaid bills.

The worst that can happen to investors in a limited liability company is that they lose their initial investment if the company fails. By limiting the downside risk for shareholders, companies can attract *equity investors* and raise large amounts of money with which to run the company. These funds are called *equity capital* and are obtained by selling shares in the company, instead of borrowing money at potentially high interest rates.

The names of companies around the world reflect this guarantee of limited liability. The abbreviations "GmbH" in Germany, "Inc." in the United States, and "Ltd." in other English-speaking countries indicate that the firm is a limited liability company, and that investors have nothing more to lose than the money invested in their shares. The "S.A." in French- and Spanish-speaking countries also refers to limited liability by defining shareholders as "anonymous." Since the identity of shareholders can be kept secret, the creditors of a bankrupt company have no right to pursue them for the company's unpaid debts.

Many countries make a clear distinction between large

and small companies, often called public and private companies, with separate designations, such as AG and GmbH in
Germany and Plc and Ltd. in Britain. Generally, "public" companies are those large enough to have their shares traded on
stock exchanges. Smaller unquoted companies are said to be
"private" even though their shares can be held by the public" at
large. In some countries, companies whose shares are not available to the general public are also called "private." In the United
States, where little distinction is made between public and private companies, most companies simply bear the title "Incorporated."

22. WHAT IS EQUITY?

OWNERSHIP IN A COMPANY, called *equity*, is certi-
fied through pieces of paper called shares or stock. These
pieces of paper state that the holder of those shares owns a part
of the company. When a company makes a profit, its owners
share in the benefits by receiving a dividend or by seeing the
shares' price go up.

There is also a risk to equity investments. When the company
loses money, the dividends are reduced or eliminated and the share
price tends to fall. In the worst case, the company goes bankrupt,
owing more than it can pay. The shares then become worthless,
and the owners often lose all of the money invested in them.

All investments involve a certain amount of risk, but a
stock is generally considered much more risky than a bond,
which is an agreement to pay a certain amount of money at a
certain time in the future.

In contrast to the "fixed income" of a bond, the return on an equity investment is unknown. To reward investors for this risk, equity tends to provide a higher return over the long term, either as a dividend payment or as an increase in the value of the shares, or both. Stocks often rise and fall in value rapidly, while bonds are generally more stable over the long term. Bondholders are creditors of a company with a guaranteed return on their investment, whereas shareholders are owners, with all the risks and rewards ownership entails.

International equity investment is not limited to the major financial centers of London, New York, and Tokyo. Equity ownership can now mean a share of a fast-food store in Moscow, a tennis shoe manufacturing plant in Thailand, or an oil company in Mexico. It can be part ownership of a hotel in Rio de Janeiro or of a light bulb company in Budapest. Equity means ownership, and ownership is now allowed in almost every country in the world.

23. WHAT IS A BALANCE SHEET?

IF A COCONUT JUICE stand on a Samoan island beach were treated as a company, its balance sheet would look like the following: its assets would be made up of the coconuts and the materials necessary to make and sell the juice, plus any cash on hand. If anything had to be borrowed to set up the operation, these debts would have to be listed as liabilities. Whatever was left over after subtracting the debts from the assets would become the budding young entrepreneur's stockholders' equity.

BALANCE SHEET
GILLIGAN'S COCONUT JUICE LTD.
(SAMOAN ISLAND BRANCH)

ASSETS		LIABILITIES	
Cash:		Debts:	
$10 in coins:	$ 10	Borrowed Knife:	$ 10
Inventory:			
10 coconuts	$ 10		
Fixed assets:			
Knife, Table:	$ 80	Stockholders' Equity:	$ 90
Total Assets:	$100	Total Liabilities:	$100

All of the assets and liabilities of a company—even one as small as a coconut stand in the South Pacific—can be added up to see what the company owes and what it owns. A *balance sheet* is simply a summary, a snapshot of a company's position at a given point in time.

A balance sheet is made up of two lists, placed side by side. On the left, the company lists everything it owns, such as cash and "fixed assets" called *property, plant, and equipment*, which include everything from buildings and trucks to tools, pencils, and copy machines. This list is labeled *assets*. On the other side, the company lists its *liabilities*, consisting of all claims to the company's assets from creditors and from the company's owners. The lists end up exactly equal—whatever assets are not claimed by the company's creditors belong to the owners.

When the company's shareholders sit down to see what they really own, they look at the lists on both sides of the balance sheet. By subtracting a company's liabilities from its assets, shareholders can calculate the *stockholders' equity* to see what belongs to them after all of the company's debts have been paid off. This is also commonly called *book value*.

When liabilities, such as loans from banks, start to exceed the level of a company's assets, the shareholders may become nervous and sell their shares. They don't want to be around on the day when the company can no longer pay its debts and is forced to declare bankruptcy, reducing the shareholders' equity to nothing.

The purpose of accounting is to provide the company's shareholders with a clear picture of a company's financial health. This "photograph," which is usually published at least once a year, can be used as a managerial tool, allowing us to see how efficiently a company is run and whether it should stay in business.

24. WHAT IS A PROFIT AND LOSS STATEMENT?

ANY ENTERPRISE, FROM a major Brazilian conglomerate to a small coconut juice stand in the middle of the South Pacific, needs a summary of what the company has earned and spent over a given period of time. This overview of a company's day-to-day activities is called an income statement or, more commonly, a *profit and loss statement (P&L)*.

A company making and selling coconut juice, for example, would start its P&L with a summary of all revenues from selling the juice. To determine its profit, the company needs to subtract its expenses from its revenues. First, it would subtract the costs incurred in producing the juice, called "cost of goods sold." Expenses such as salaries or maintenance of assets would also have to be accounted for. Other expenses, such as interest on loans, would then have to be deducted. Finally, *depreciation*, the decline in value of fixed assets, such as machinery and tools, would have to be deducted from earnings.

PROFIT AND LOSS STATEMENT
GILLIGAN'S COCONUT JUICE LTD.
(SAMOAN ISLAND BRANCH)

PERIOD: ONE YEAR

Revenues (from sale of coconut juice):	$50
Cost of Goods Sold (paid to coconut pickers):	$10
Other Expenses (advertising on beach):	$10
Gross Profit	$30
Taxes (33% rate)	$10
Net Profit:	$20

Depreciation causes many accounting nightmares because it is difficult to determine how much a fixed asset really declines in value over time. Many companies take advantage of this uncertainty to show as much "loss" as possible, reducing earnings in order to pay less tax in the early years of the asset's life. By delaying tax payments, companies can earn valuable interest on their retained earnings.

Once all expenses have been deducted from the revenues, a company sees its total profit or loss. This is the proverbial "bottom line." It tells us how much the company's assets and liabilities changed over the course of the year.

Another tool for understanding a company's activity is to look at its *cash flow*. This is like a profit and loss statement, except that it only measures the actual flow of funds—real money—moving into and out of a company during a given period. A company's cash flow, or "cash summary," factors out all of the accounting tricks and looks at what a company really earned. Even though cash flow does not tell us the company's "profit," cash flow sometimes gives a clearer picture of a company's true earnings, because it excludes the hard-to-quantify items such as depreciation.

Cash flows and profit and loss statements are essential for understanding the revenues, expenses, and profits of any organization, including nonprofit organizations such as the World Wildlife Fund or the United Nations. Even if profits are not distributed to shareholders, any organization needs a P&L to account for its activities to see whether it is being efficiently and honestly run.

25. WHAT IS NET WORTH?

THE TOTAL MONETARY value of a company or individual, anywhere in the world, is called *net worth*. An individual's net worth, for example, is calculated by adding up assets such as houses and bank accounts, and subtracting liabilities such as mortgages and credit card bills.

The net worth of a company is calculated in the same way as for an individual, subtracting its liabilities from its assets. On a balance sheet, a company's net worth is called *shareholders' equity*.

Problems arise when a company's balance sheet includes intangible assets, such as brand names, that cannot be treated as a normal asset. Most accountants call these assets *goodwill*, although the term rarely refers to any good deeds or charitable efforts of the company. The extra price paid to purchase a well-known law firm, for example, would be called goodwill by accountants. Other examples of goodwill are the extra value in a brand name or a good reputation. Although hard to quantify, intangible assets can be sold just like other assets.

Since goodwill and other nontangible assets are so difficult to value, many analysts prefer to exclude them when calculating what a company is really worth, subtracting liabilities from tangible assets such as cash, buildings, and equipment. In this way, the company's *tangible net worth* provides a more conservative estimate of the company's value.

Net worth is also called *book value* because it shows what would be left on the books if the company were to be liquidated. In a liquidation, a company sells off all of its assets—such as buildings, computers, and bonds—and pays off all of its liabilities—such as bills, bank loans, and mortgages.

In the mergers and acquisitions world, the wheeler-dealers look at a company's net worth to see what profit can be made from selling off the company's assets. A company could be valued more than its net worth, however, if it has a strong potential for growth, a good worldwide reputation, or a particular expertise in a foreign market.

26. HOW ARE COMPANIES COMPARED INTERNATIONALLY?

LIKE A FRUIT tree with many years of harvests to come, the value of a company's shares is based on what the company is worth now and what it can provide in earnings in the years to come. A company's earnings, similar to a fruit tree's annual production of oranges or pears, are accounted for at the end of each year.

A company's share price is often based on its earnings, usually as a ratio, called the *price/earnings (p/e) ratio*. When a company's earnings increase, its share price usually rises, keeping its p/e ratio in line with other companies within its industry. A company with a price/earnings ratio of 10/1, for example, has a share price ten times the amount the company earns per share per year, implying that the stock would pay for itself in ten years' time.

The problem in comparing p/e ratios from country to country is that each country has its own accounting rules: earnings may be understated in one country and overstated in another. It is hard to judge a company's value when the measuring sticks are not the same. Instead of asking, "Is the price too high?" it may be more relevant to ask, "Are the reported earnings too low?"

In Japan, for example, different accounting rules allow many Japanese companies to report fewer earnings than would be accounted for by European or North American standards. In Japan, most companies hold stock in other companies. The earnings from many of these holdings are not included in their reported earnings. The 5 percent stake that Mitsubishi Trust may hold in Kirin Breweries would be reflected in its price per share but not in its earnings statement. Japanese price/earnings ratios, therefore, often look high by Western standards.

Similarly, many Japanese companies use an "accelerated depreciation" method to show lower profits in the early years of an asset's life, a practice that is not allowed in most Western countries. If the Japanese were to use Western depreciation methods, their reported earnings would rise considerably. These differences in accounting practices lead many big international investors to do their own financial analysis of companies around the world, recalculating foreign companies' earnings according to a common set of accounting rules. This recalculation often brings foreign p/e ratios in line with those of other companies in the world economy.

27. WHAT IS A LEVERAGED BUYOUT?

BY USING FORCE at the right point, you can use a playground seesaw to lift a large weight with a relatively small amount of strength. Similarly, a *leveraged buyout* (LBO) uses a relatively small investment to buy a company, usually by borrowing most of the purchase amount.

The key to any LBO is to use other people's money as a "lever" to purchase a company and then quickly recover the funds to pay off the loans. This is often accomplished by forcing the management to sell off assets and restructure the firm. The goal is to end up controlling a leaner, more profitable company.

A leveraged buyout takes advantage of the fact that a company is essentially owned by its shareholders, not its managers. Just as a bank president does not own the bank, a company's managers do not own the company, the shareholders do—and anyone who owns enough shares can take over a company. When an investor, or a group of investors, thinks the company can be run better by a new group of managers, it can attempt a takeover. If the company's management opposes the goals of the new controlling shareholders, it becomes a "hostile takeover."

LBO specialists normally buy undervalued companies that own a large amount of underperforming assets such as cash, real estate, or other holdings. By breaking up the company and selling off valuable assets, in a process called *asset stripping*, the mountain of debt used to acquire the company can be paid off. Many successful LBOs have been financed by *junk bonds*, high-yield securities that attract investors because of the high interest rates paid to those willing to take a risk on the LBO's success. If the LBO fails, however, the high interest payments may stop and the bonds literally become junk.

How can a company's management ward off hostile takeovers? A company can be restructured, or assets can be sold off, making the company unattractive for the takeover artists. Other *poison pill* defenses may include buying back the company's shares in the open market, driving up the price and making the company too expensive for a takeover. After the LBO fad spread internationally in the early 1990s, many European and Japanese companies asked their governments to erect new barriers with laws designed to limit the power of "foreigners" to acquire local companies.

Sometimes managers may decide to get into the LBO game

as well, deciding, "if you can't beat 'em, join 'em." In a *management buyout*, the management itself arranges to take over the company themselves, often borrowing enormous amounts of money to buy a controlling number of the company's shares.

When a leveraged buyout works, the shareholders are better off, and the company ends up being more efficient and more valuable. If it doesn't work—with the debt load weighing too heavily on profits—a company can be destroyed. When it cannot pay its new debts on time, for example, a formerly profitable company acquired through a leveraged buyout can be forced to declare bankruptcy.

28. HOW DO COMPANIES IN THE GLOBAL ECONOMY TRANSCEND NATIONAL BOUNDARIES?

ONE OF THE goals of the environmental movement, "Think Globally, Act Locally," is rapidly being achieved by international businesses. Just as state power has crumbled in the face of global trade and multinational political blocs, such companies as Sony, Motorola, Ford, Nestlé, and Coca-Cola have decentralized decision-making, leaving behind corporate headquarters that merely coordinate the locally managed activities of operations abroad.

At IBM, for example, each foreign subsidiary has its own culture, its own local way of doing things. The corporate headquarters in the United States were progressively reduced, "downsized," to serve as a central clearing house to which the hundreds of foreign and domestic profit centers report their results. Management of each of these profit centers is increasingly left to the local directors. In this way, a Japanese client of IBM sees the Tokyo office as essentially a Japanese company; a German client would perceive the Frankfurt IBM office to be essentially German. This scenario is repeated throughout the globe: from Buenos Aires to Bombay, IBM has "devoluted" the decision-making power to locally managed offices.

The same process is being used by almost every multinational company. These companies could, in fact, be called "supranational." Nestlé, Switzerland's biggest food company, is perceived by many people in the United States to be an American company, and in Brazil as Brazilian. By the 1990s, Nestlé's sales of chocolate, milk, and food products were derived almost entirely from outside Switzerland.

Another example is *Readers Digest*, with many editions in several different languages around the world. Readers in Mexico read locally written stories in Spanish, and readers in Austria read them in German. Other publications, such as *Playboy* and *Cosmopolitan*, have also seen sales boom after launching local editions around the world, with a mix of local and international stories—and centerfolds.

Just as products have become global, tastes in products have converged. A Brazilian may actually prefer to eat at McDonald's rather than at a Churrascaria; an American may prefer Absolut Vodka to Southern Comfort; an Italian may prefer a BMW to a Ferrari. Among the most famous brand names on the face of the planet, Coca-Cola, Marlboro, Sony, and Levi's all have aficionados in almost every country in the world economy. Many of these brands now produce "global" commercials with only small changes to adapt them to local markets.

Ford, almost from its beginning, has been a global company. By the 1920s, Fords were rolling off assembly lines in countries around the world, in such locations as Argentina, Mexico, Australia—and even Japan. Ford now designs several cars as "world cars" with parts and assembly coming from all corners of the globe.

As the world economy integrates, it is becoming increasingly difficult to "buy local." What's an "American" car? A Honda that's built in Ohio by a Japanese company? Or a Ford assembled in Brazil with parts from Europe and the United States? Conversely, what is Japanese beef? If the cows in Japan are fed a steady diet of American grain, are they not more American than Japanese?

Entertainment is also becoming a global industry. In Hollywood, by the beginning of the 1990s, half the revenue earned by movies was coming from outside the United States. And of the six major record companies in the United States only one was not in foreign hands. With MTV broadcasting around the world, and with local radio stations beaming a steady stream of English-language music to teenagers from Croatia to Chile, music has truly become a global industry.

For example, more than half of the songs played on the radio in Brazil, Germany, or Japan are in English. But how many U.S. teenagers know, or care, that many English-language songs they hear are actually sung by foreign groups? At the same time, U.S. rock superstars from Michael Jackson to Madonna have often been more popular in many foreign countries than in the United States. By the mid-1990s, MTV was being beamed to more than 200 million households in more than 70 countries around the world, using different formats and languages to suit the local markets.

Sony's decision to buy CBS Records was motivated by the

promised access to the "global" entertainment industry. Sony wanted the software to play on its hardware, so it purchased the record company, which had an extensive library of rock music and recording artists. Sony's strategy was to decentralize authority to several centers scattered around the world, called "global localization." Its sales of electronics had already followed this global theme. The Sony Walkman, one of the most ubiquitous entertainment devices in the world, could be found by the 1990s in any back street of any Third World country. In fact, many customers around the world neither know, nor care, that Sony is a Japanese company. In the new global economy, companies want to resemble insiders, no matter where they may operate.

29. HOW ARE INTERNATIONAL INVESTMENTS COMPARED?

LIKE COMPARING APPLES and oranges, comparing the return of international investments can be a daunting task. How can an investment in Japanese stocks be compared to an investment in silver bullion? How can the purchase of Mexican real estate be compared to the purchase of a mutual fund based on U.S. Treasury bonds?

Just as various fruits can be compared by weight, international investments can be evaluated by their total return, or *yield*, which includes the total increase in value plus any dividends or other payments. College endowment funds, insurance companies, banks, and individual investors usually base their evaluations on one accepted currency, U.S. dollars for example, to compare their growing portfolios of global investments.

The return on any investment—from stocks and commodities to art and real estate—can be evaluated by looking at its yield: the percentage increase in value over a given period. In this way, a Canadian fund for widows and orphans that invests in an emerging market, with a 600 percent increase in value over a ten-year period, can distribute much more money to its clients than if the fund had invested in the U.S. money market, perhaps yielding only 150 percent over the same ten-year period.

Yield, however, is only one factor to consider in evaluating international investments. A prudent investor has to consider a wide range of variables, including tax considerations and political risk, when contemplating any foray into the world of global finance.

30. WHAT ARE THE RISKS OF INTERNATIONAL INVESTING?

INTERNATIONAL INVESTING IS a risky business. When the communist economies of Eastern Europe were transformed into free-market economies, for example, their credit risks improved immeasurably, and those who moved in early often saw the value of their investments flourish. In some countries, however, investors were not so lucky, as political turmoil and economic chaos pushed many ventures to the brink of bankruptcy.

International investing carries additional risks along with additional rewards. Global investors—from first-time individuals to experienced pension funds—need to look very carefully at each country's political and economic situation before sending their money abroad.

By identifying—and possibly removing—some of the risks involved, the wheel of fortune of the global markets can actually spin in the investor's favor. Banks, for example, have made a science of weighing the risks in international investment. When lending money to international borrowers, they not only consider the traditional "domestic" risks of credit, maturity, interest rates, and so forth, but they identify additional hazards, such as *exchange risk* and *political risk*.

Exchange risk—changes in the value of foreign currencies—can sometimes work in the investor's favor, providing additional profits if the foreign currency gains in value. On the other hand, if the foreign currency plummets, the loss could eat away the earnings from an otherwise lucrative international investment. A California employees' fund that invests in Tokyo, for example, may see the value of its stocks and bonds rising handsomely as the Japanese markets boom, but if the yen loses value against the U.S. dollar, those foreign "earnings" may end up being a loss for those who need the money at home.

On the other hand, a foreign investor stands to gain handsomely if the yen increases in value against the home currency. The profit from an investment in a strong foreign currency can sometimes exceed the profit from increases in value of the investment itself.

International investments also entail political risk if the government falls or new laws are passed restricting international transfers. If a democratically elected government is toppled by a military coup, for example, the local markets may drop like a stone as foreign investment money flees the country. A stable government that ensures international payments is an important requirement for any global investment.

The advice of ratings agencies and global political analysts—now fairly common in most business magazines—can also help calculate international risk. After all the risks have been calculated, international investment can provide a return that will reward the investor for the various risks taken.

STOCK MARKET INDEXES AND AVERAGES FROM AROUND THE WORLD

Argentina, Buenos Aires: General Index
Australia, Sydney: All Ordinaries Index
Austria, Vienna: ATX Index (Austrian Traded Index)
Belgium, Brussels: Bel-20 Index
Brazil, São Paulo: Bovespa Index (Bolsa de Valores de São Paulo)
Britain, London: FT-SE 100 (Financial Times—Stock Exchange 100-Share Index)
Canada, Toronto: TSE 300 Index (Toronto Stock Exchange 300 Composite Index)
Denmark, Copenhagen: Stock Market Index
France, Paris: CAC-40 Index
Finland, Helsinki: HEX General Index
Germany, Frankfurt: DAX Index (Deutscher Aktien-Index)
Hong Kong: Hang Seng Index
India, Bombay: Bombay Stock Exchange Sensitive Index
Indonesia, Jakarta: Composite Index
Italy, Milan: MIB Telematico Index
Japan, Tokyo: Nikkei 225-Stock Index
Malaysia, Kuala Lumpur: Composite Index
Mexico, Mexico City: Bolsa Index
Netherlands, Amsterdam: EOE Index (European Options Exchange Index)
New Zealand, Wellington: NZSE-40 Index (New Zealand Stock Exchange 40-Shares Index)

Norway, Oslo: OBX Industrial Index
Philippines, Manila: PSE Index (Philippines Stock Exchange Index)
Singapore: Straits Times Index
South Africa, Johannesburg: All Market Index
Spain, Madrid: Madrid Stock Exchange Index
South Korea, Seoul: Composite Index
Sweden, Stockholm: Affarsvarlden General Index
Switzerland, Zurich: SPI (Swiss Performance Index)
Taiwan, Taipei: Stock Market Index
Thailand, Bangkok: SET Index (Stock Exchange of Thailand Index)
United States, New York: Dow Jones Industrial Average; Standard & Poor's 500
    Index
Global: MSCI (Morgan Stanley Capital International World Index);
    Trib Index (International Herald Tribune World Stock Index)

31. WHAT IS A STOCK INDEX?

IT IS NOT necessary for a farmer to examine every plant in the field to see how a crop is growing. It is usually sufficient to look at a few plants to get a good idea of the progress of the crop as a whole. Likewise, an investor does not have to look at every stock traded to see where the market moved on a particular day. It is usually sufficient to look at the prices of a small group of stocks, making up an *index*, which is used to represent the stock market as a whole.

Every major stock market has at least one index that tracks the movements of a group of representative stocks. The Dow Jones Industrial Average, for example, tracks the prices of thirty of the most prestigious "blue-chip" stocks on the New York Stock Exchange (NYSE), America's biggest stock market. Sometimes it is more useful to look at a broader index that takes the weighted average of hundreds of shares. The Standard & Poor's (S&P) 500, for example, measures the movement of five hundred different stocks on the NYSE.

The prices of the shares in each group are usually indexed, giving more weight to the price change in stocks of larger companies such as IBM or Nippon Telephone & Telegraph. There are exceptions, such as the Nikkei-Dow Jones Index in Tokyo that simply averages the prices of every stock in the group, regardless of its relative importance to the market.

In most countries, a group of stocks is chosen by a major bank—or sometimes a news agency, such as Dow Jones in New York—to provide investors with a measure of the market's activities on any particular day. In Japan, for example, the Nikkei Index receives its name from the acronym of Japan's leading financial newspaper, the *Nihon Keizai Shimbun*. In London, the name of the major stock index refers to the newspaper *The Financial Times*. In most other European countries, banks, such as Credit Suisse in Zurich or Banca Commerciale Italiana in Milan, provide stock indexes that bear their names.

32. HOW DO INVESTORS BUY FOREIGN SHARES?

A S FOREIGN MARKETS have expanded their role in the world economy, many investors have begun to invest in foreign stocks. International investors can now buy shares of almost any company in the world, including those in the growing economies of Eastern Europe and the Far East.

One way to invest in foreign companies is simply to buy the shares on the foreign market through a broker. Toyota shares in Japan or Club Med shares in France, for example, can be bought in Tokyo or Paris by a local broker and deposited in a normal brokerage account anywhere in the world. But the foreign share's price is still quoted on a foreign exchange and dividends are still paid in a foreign currency. Most foreign investors would have a hard time reading a Japanese or French newspaper to keep track of their stocks.

To avoid many of the inconveniences of owning shares in foreign countries, many companies have decided to have their shares listed as certificates on stock exchanges around the world. All of the payments and prices for these certificates are listed in the local currency. Just as a credit card purchase abroad is translated into the card holder's home currency, these certificates allow investors to pay for foreign shares with their own currencies.

These foreign stock certificates give the holder the rights to a foreign share, called an *underlying share*. When the foreign share changes its value, its stock certificate on the other side of the world also changes its value. For example, North American investors can buy a Japanese or a French stock as an ADR, an American Depository Receipt, which gives them the rights to the foreign shares. In this way, the buyer of an ADR for Toyota does not have to keep track of the yen price of the shares. The ADR price is in dollars on North American exchanges and dividends are also credited in dollars directly to the owner's account.

Currency risks still have to be considered, because the certificate's value also depends on the currency exchange rate. If the foreign currency goes up in value, the owner of the certificate will benefit. If Toyota stock goes down, for example, a Californian owning a Toyota ADR might still make money if the Japanese yen improves against the dollar sufficiently to offset the decline in stock value.

In other countries, where foreign ownership of shares is prohibited or extremely difficult, investors may want to buy shares in a *country fund*. In South Korea, for example, before direct foreign ownership was allowed, various funds were set up to allow foreign investors to profit from the rises in the South Korean stock market.

Besides traditional *registered shares*, some countries, such as Switzerland, offer investors the choice of *bearer shares*, which do not require registering the owners' names. Other investment possibilities include *participation certificates*, which provide dividends like other shares but do not allow the investor to vote at stockholders' meetings and make decisions on running the company.

33. WHAT IS AN EQUITY FUND?

INSTEAD OF PUTTING all of their eggs in one basket, international investors often buy equity funds that spread the risk over a wide range of stocks. Equity funds essentially allow investors to avoid the pain of losing all of their money on one bankrupt company. The funds are made up of a group of different securities, such as stocks and stock options, that are bought and sold for the fund by professional fund managers.

Many international investors prefer to leave the decisions on foreign equity investment to these highly skilled fund managers. In theory, they can understand the individual markets better and are better able to avoid costly mistakes. By buying a share in an equity fund, such as a "Far East fund" or a "growth stock fund," investors can diversify their risk. If any one company in an equity fund goes bankrupt, each investor suffers minimal loss because of the other healthy companies in the fund.

Politically or socially conscious investors, such as college endowment funds or concerned individuals, may prefer to invest in equity funds that correspond to their economic and political goals. A fund that invests only in companies that protect the environment, for example, or one that avoids companies using child labor in the Third World, allows investors to accomplish specific social goals with their money.

There are many different equity funds available for the international investor. *Growth stock funds* invest primarily in companies that retain their earnings and concentrate on rapid growth. In an *income stock fund*, investments are made primarily in already-established companies that pay consistent dividends. This type of investment may be of interest to a pension fund, for example, which needs a fixed income for payments to retired people. A *country fund* provides investors with an opportunity to share in the growth of specific foreign markets.

There are two types of structures for equity funds. A "closed-end" investment fund (called an "investment trust" in Britain) has a limited number of shares available. These shares trade on the open markets, where their price is determined by supply and demand. In an "open-end" investment fund (called a "unit trust" in Britain) new shares are simply issued whenever a new investor wants in, and the price is not determined by supply and demand but by the value of the fund's holdings.

34. WHAT IS BANKRUPTCY?

THE TERM *BANKRUPTCY* is based on the practice of breaking the bench of traders in medieval Italy who were not able to pay their debts. Once a trader's bench (banco) was "ruptured," it was impossible to continue operations. Today, a bankrupt company has a choice: it may liquidate its assets immediately or it may be allowed to attempt a recovery under a supervised legal framework.

The capitalist system uses the lure of profits to attract investors to a new venture, and the fear of bankruptcy forces companies to be run properly. A company's stockholders share in the glory and the pain of both extremes. When a company makes a profit, the shareholders receive a dividend or enjoy the rise in value of a company's stocks. When the company loses money, however, shareholders also lose as the company's stocks decline in value.

If an ailing company loses so much money that it cannot pay its debts, it declares bankruptcy, forcing it and its creditors to find a solution. Shareholders see their investment dwindle and even disappear as creditors, such as suppliers and bondholders, are paid off with whatever funds are available.

In most capitalist countries, bankrupt companies are first encouraged to try to continue operating under legal supervision in order to generate enough money to pay off creditors. Like having a mechanic fix a broken-down car instead of sending it to the junk heap, a company can sometimes be given a new life through this court-appointed restructuring. Rehabilitation, called "Chapter Eleven" in the United States or "administration" in Britain, gives an insolvent company the opportunity to reorganize and possibly return to profitability.

If a company shows no real prospect of recovering, it is forced into liquidation, called "Chapter Seven" in the United States or "receivership" in Britain. Under liquidation, assets are sold off to provide enough funds to pay off at least part of a company's debts. The various terms for bankruptcy used around the world are:

COUNTRY	REHABILITATION	LIQUIDATION
United States	Chapter Eleven	Chapter Seven
Britain, Canada	Administration	Receivership
France	Règlement à l'amiable	Liquidation
Germany	Vergleich	Konkurs
Italy	Amministrazione	Liquidazione
Japan	Kaishakoseiho	Tosan

35. WHAT IS A CAPITAL MARKET?

INSTEAD OF BORROWING money from a bank, governments and other creditworthy borrowers such as companies and international agencies often use the world's capital markets to get money for their operations. This is usually done by issuing bonds and other debt instruments. In most cases, this allows them to raise funds at a lower cost than by borrowing directly from a bank.

The international capital markets are used for issuing and trading the world's securities, pieces of paper representing value. These pieces of paper could be anything from a bond to a financial future.

There is no one center for capital market trading, but a series of electronically linked markets: banks and trading floors located in cities all over the world, from Tokyo and Singapore to London and New York, to name just a few. The international capital markets serve one main purpose: they transfer money from those who have it to those who need it and are willing to pay a price to get it. Hundreds of billions, if not trillions, of dollars—and marks, yen, pounds, and francs—are traded daily on capital markets around the world.

Capital, accumulated wealth, forms the basis for all economic activity in market-oriented, or *capitalist*, societies. In this sense, capital markets should not be confused with the machinery and buildings, also called capital, which a company uses to produce goods and services.

The debt instruments traded on the world's capital markets can be bought and sold just like any other commodity. The price borrowers pay for money, represented by pieces of paper called securities, is the interest rate. This price, or interest rate, is determined by supply and demand. When there is a shortage of money to lend, borrowers have to pay a higher interest rate. When money is plentiful, interest rates decline.

The international capital markets bring together a wide range of borrowers and lenders. Investors in the world's capital markets can be as large as the California state pension fund trading in Tokyo and London or as small as a Swiss farmer wanting to buy securities at a local bank. Borrowers include corporations, institutions, and governments—which as IBM, the World Bank, or the Kingdom of Sweden—which issue bonds and securities on the world's capital markets on a daily basis.

When a Swiss investor buys bonds
ment Bank or a Japanese pension fund
bonds, money is transferred from <
another, where it can be used for devel<
the interlinked global economy, savings do no<
under a mattress, but can be invested through the intern<
capital markets to be used productively around the world.

36. WHAT IS A BOND?

UNLIKE A STOCK, which represents the risk and reward of ownership in a company, a bond is simply a loan agreement that says: "I, the borrower, agree to pay to you, the bondholder, a certain amount of money at a certain time in the future." Basically, anyone can issue a bond, as long as someone is willing to buy it.

The buyer of the bond, who is essentially lending money to the issuer, has to have confidence that the bond will be paid back at some time in the future, along with the agreed amount of interest. Governments and corporations are the world's biggest issuers of bonds. Instead of turning to a bank to lend them money, they issue bonds to raise large sums of money, often as global issues of securities sold to banks and other investors around the world.

A bond is basically an IOU, a piece of paper giving the holder the right to receive a specific amount of money in the future. The borrower, or issuer, of a bond, has two obligations.

he issuer has to pay back the original amount borrowed, d the *principal*. Second, the borrower needs to pay interest iodically, to reward those who buy the bond as an invest- ment. These interest payments are also called *coupons*. This term was derived from the little pieces of paper attached to the bonds before the electronic markets made such paper transac- tions unnecessary.

How do you determine the value of a bond? It is first nec- essary to calculate the interest paid over the bond's life. This "re- turn" is then compared to other interest-bearing investments in the marketplace. Bond prices are constantly raised or lowered to reflect this market analysis.

Essentially, bond prices follow interest rates. A bond pay- ing a relatively low rate of interest, therefore, will be sold at a discount when higher-interest bonds are issued by the same type of borrower. A low-coupon bond, for example, may have to be sold for 90 percent of its face value, or redemption value, to make it attractive enough to compete with other bonds with higher interest rates. In paying less for a bond, the buyer receives a higher return, or *yield*, on the amount invested. Like a play- ground seesaw, when one side—price—goes down, the other side—yield—goes up.

Conversely, when interest rates fall, the prices of existing bonds rise. In a period of declining interest rates, for example, a relatively high-coupon bond would see its price increase, until its yield is the same as other bonds in the market with similar maturity and similar risk. A bond's price may easily rise above its face value, to 110 percent, for example, to make its yield com- petitive with other bonds in the market.

Interest rates and bond prices are also determined by the bond's risk—the likelihood of the bond being repaid: the riskier the bond, the higher the interest a potential borrower will have

When a Swiss investor buys bonds of the African Development Bank or a Japanese pension fund invests in U.S. Treasury bonds, money is transferred from one part of the world to another, where it can be used for development and growth. In the interlinked global economy, savings do not have to be kept under a mattress, but can be invested through the international capital markets to be used productively around the world.

36. WHAT IS A BOND?

UNLIKE A STOCK, which represents the risk and reward of ownership in a company, a bond is simply a loan agreement that says: "I, the borrower, agree to pay to you, the bond-holder, a certain amount of money at a certain time in the future." Basically, anyone can issue a bond, as long as someone is willing to buy it.

The buyer of the bond, who is essentially lending money to the issuer, has to have confidence that the bond will be paid back at some time in the future, along with the agreed amount of interest. Governments and corporations are the world's biggest issuers of bonds. Instead of turning to a bank to lend them money, they issue bonds to raise large sums of money, often as global issues of securities sold to banks and other investors around the world.

A bond is basically an IOU, a piece of paper giving the holder the right to receive a specific amount of money in the future. The borrower, or issuer, of a bond, has two obligations.

First the issuer has to pay back the original amount borrowed, called the *principal*. Second, the borrower needs to pay interest periodically, to reward those who buy the bond as an investment. These interest payments are also called *coupons*. This term was derived from the little pieces of paper attached to the bonds before the electronic markets made such paper transactions unnecessary.

How do you determine the value of a bond? It is first necessary to calculate the interest paid over the bond's life. This "return" is then compared to other interest-bearing investments in the marketplace. Bond prices are constantly raised or lowered to reflect this market analysis.

Essentially, bond prices follow interest rates. A bond paying a relatively low rate of interest, therefore, will be sold at a discount when higher-interest bonds are issued by the same type of borrower. A low-coupon bond, for example, may have to be sold for 90 percent of its face value, or redemption value, to make it attractive enough to compete with other bonds with higher interest rates. In paying less for a bond, the buyer receives a higher return, or *yield*, on the amount invested. Like a playground seesaw, when one side—price—goes down, the other side—yield—goes up.

Conversely, when interest rates fall, the prices of existing bonds rise. In a period of declining interest rates, for example, a relatively high-coupon bond would see its price increase, until its yield is the same as other bonds in the market with similar maturity and similar risk. A bond's price may easily rise above its face value, to 110 percent, for example, to make its yield competitive with other bonds in the market.

Interest rates and bond prices are also determined by the bond's risk—the likelihood of the bond being repaid: the riskier the bond, the higher the interest a potential borrower will have to pay to attract investors. A Brazilian sugar company with a higher risk of going bankrupt than a sovereign government would therefore have to pay a higher interest rate than the government of Sweden for bonds with a similar maturity.

Bonds, especially government bonds, are seen to be a relatively safe investment. In the worst-case scenario, of a company going bankrupt for example, the bondholders get paid before the stockholders. A government bond in its own national currency has the least risk because, in a worst-case scenario, a government can pay off bonds by simply printing more money.

Bond prices are adjusted on an ongoing basis, allowing them to compete with other investments in the global economy, always reflecting the current political, monetary, and economic environment.

37. HOW ARE BONDS TRADED?

TWENTY-FOUR HOURS A DAY, bonds are traded around the world—usually in trading rooms of banks and securities houses, which are connected by elaborate systems of electronic communications equipment. The largest international capital markets are based in London, New York, and Tokyo, but bonds are traded in almost every financial center in the world, from Paris to Bangkok, from Johannesburg to Vancouver.

Since it is difficult for bond investors to find individual sellers, they usually go to professional "market-makers" who buy and sell their bonds for them. Although some bond trading takes place on public trading floors such as stock exchanges, most of the world's fixed-income securities are traded by banks and securities houses acting as market-makers on behalf of their clients. Bond markets are just like any other competitive market in that traders make money by buying for less and selling for more.

How do you sell a bond? An investor wanting to sell a bond would go through a broker to a trader who makes a "market" with two prices: a "bid" price and an "offer" price. The investor sells bonds to the trader at the "bid" price, which is always lower than the "offer" price. The difference between the two prices is called the *spread*. A trader makes money in small amounts all day long, buying at the lower bid price and selling at the slightly higher offer price.

Bond traders are forced by the market to keep their prices and spreads competitive. A trader with bid prices that are too low and offer prices that are too high will lose business to other traders in the markets with better prices or narrower spreads. Some markets are so competitive that the bid and offer prices are quoted in tiny fractions of a percent. In the government bond markets, for example, prices are given as 1/32nds of a percentage point.

Bonds are usually traded with prices based on a percentage of their original face value. When the price of a thousand-dollar bond rises by 16/32, or one-half of one percent, its value increases by five dollars. Since the original value of the bond and its interest rates normally do not change, adjusting the bond's price is the only way to give it a new yield. These bond yield calculations are so complex that most traders use calculators to determine the prices and yields, keeping them in line with the changing market.

In the international capital markets, some bonds—such as

U.S. Treasury bonds—serve as "bellwether" indicators of the market as a whole. Because of the enormous amount of U.S. Treasury debt issued, international investors use this market for a large part of their trading and investing. U.S., British, and German government securities are said to be the most *liquid* bonds in the world, because they can be traded internationally at almost any given time.

38. WHAT ARE EUROCURRENCIES AND EUROBONDS?

DURING THE COLD war, the Soviet Union was reluctant to put its U.S. dollar reserves under the control of authorities in the United States. Instead of putting its dollar deposits in New York banks, it turned to European banks to keep those dollars abroad, and those reserves became known as *Eurodollars*. Today, any currency held abroad, even outside Europe, is called a *Eurocurrency*. Japanese yen held in a New York bank, for example, are called Euroyen, and French francs being held in a Hong Kong bank are called Eurofrancs.

By the 1970s and 1980s, a huge market had developed for Eurocurrencies. Arab oil producers, following the example of the Soviet Union, began keeping a large part of their newly earned "petrodollars" in European banks. This flood of foreign capital needed to be invested, so European-based banks began issuing U.S. dollar bonds, outside the control and regulations of the United States government. These bonds were called Eurobonds because they, like Eurocurrencies, were issued and held outside the country of their currency. The world's banks and securities houses then began issuing Eurobonds in all of the world's major currencies, such as Japanese yen, German marks, Austrian dollars, Canadian dollars and French francs.

The Eurobond market grew enormously during the 1980s. Money began to pour into these unregulated "foreign" markets, settling mainly in London, where taxes and restrictions on trading were minimal. Investors also liked the fact that most Eurobonds were *bearer bonds*. Unlike registered bonds, bearer bonds allow investors to remain anonymous—usually without withholding taxes on the interest income—allowing some investors to avoid reporting the interest earnings to tax authorities at home.

When American corporations found they could issue bonds more cheaply in the Eurobond market, with lower interest rates and with fewer restrictions than in the United States, London-based Eurobond activity grew rapidly. Companies and governments from around the world began issuing many of their securities in the Eurobond market, often at less cost than in their home markets.

39. HOW ARE RATINGS USED TO EVALUATE INVESTMENTS?

EXAMINING THE FINANCIAL documents of companies from around the world would be difficult for any investor, no matter how knowledgeable. Many investors, therefore, have come to rely on the judgment of ratings agencies that make it their job to evaluate the financial health of borrowers in the world economy.

The first question an investor asks when lending money, whether to an individual, a company, or a government, is "Will they be able to pay the money back?" A bond investor, for example, needs to know whether the interest on the "loan" will be paid on time and whether the principal—the amount of money originally borrowed—will be repaid at all.

Ratings agencies use various systems, usually based on the letters A through D, to rate the world's companies and governments. Two of the world's biggest ratings agencies, Moody's Investors Services and Standard & Poor's (S&P) both provide a "Triple A" rating for the most healthy borrowers. Loans to "AAA" borrowers, such as the United States, Switzerland, Japan, or the World Bank, are considered to offer the best chance of being paid back with timely interest payments. Duff & Phelps, another ratings agency, also uses AAA, while A.M. Best uses school-style letters like A+ to denote the best borrowers.

When a borrower's financial health declines, the agencies downgrade its rating to keep investors informed of the debt's new risks. Most international funds will not invest in bonds with ratings lower than "A" or "BBB," usually called *investment grade*. When a failing borrower begins missing interest payments, its ratings will fall to "C" or lower. A rating of "D" indicates bankruptcy.

A borrower's ratings can also be upgraded when its financial health improves. As Argentina and Brazil began to recover from the severe debt crises of the 1980s, for example, the ratings on their new and existing debt were increased accordingly.

Investors accept low interest payments only from the highly rated borrowers. For this reason, most borrowers take the ratings very seriously: top-rated borrowers, such as Switzerland and Japan, can issue bonds with significantly lower interest rates, greatly reducing the cost of borrowing. Developing countries with lower ratings usually have to pay higher interest rates to investors to reward them for the additional risk of their bonds.

40. HOW IS GOLD USED AS AN INTERNATIONAL INVESTMENT?

WHETHER IN A Cairo souk or in the sophisticated commodity exchanges of Hong Kong or Chicago, gold is bought and sold in almost every market and currency imaginable.

Although some gold trading is based on commercial transactions, such as an Amsterdam jeweler buying gold for inventory, most gold is purchased as an investment. Gold investors range from powerful central banks who use gold to shore up their currencies to individuals who buy gold hoping that it will hold its value in inflationary times.

Gold's role in the world economy has changed over the years. Before banks and securities houses became part of the electronically connected "global village," gold served as a uniquely liquid investment that could be exchanged anywhere in the world at any given time. Now, gold is perceived mostly as a "hedge"—providing a stable refuge for investors in inflationary times, when financial instruments such as stocks or bonds tend to lose their value. If inflation is brought under control, however, gold loses its luster: unlike most other investments, there is no interest paid on gold. The only possible profit is its rise in value, called *capital gain*.

There are several ways of investing in gold, including buying shares in gold mining companies or gold mutual funds. Most gold investments, however, are "spot" purchases for immediate delivery. Gold is usually held in a custodian bank that charges a fee for storage, a form of "negative interest rate." Purchases are usually made in commodity exchanges, such as the Comex in New York, or in many international banks, such as Credit Suisse in Zurich, where trades are executed electronically for clients around the world.

Instead of buying "spot" gold for immediate delivery, investors can make an agreement to buy gold at a future date. These purchases are called *futures contracts* because they are based on periodic delivery dates in the future, usually every three months. Tailor-made futures contracts, with flexible dates to fit the needs of buyers and sellers, are called *forward contracts*.

Gold spot and futures prices, like a child riding piggyback, tend to move in the same direction, rising and falling with other precious metals in the market. If gold's spot price increases, its futures price usually rises accordingly. In general, the prices of precious metals such as gold, silver, and platinum tend to rise and fall in tandem.

41. WHAT ARE DERIVATIVES?

IT MAY SOUND like a house of cards, but many financial instruments in the global economy can be based on nothing more than the value of other financial instruments. When the value of the underlying instrument changes—this could be a stock quoted in Tokyo, a bond traded in London, or a pork belly contract traded in Chicago—the derivative's value also changes.

Financial instruments like stock options, financial futures, and interest rate swaps are called derivatives because their value is derived from another piece of paper. A *stock option*, for example, is called a derivative because its value is "derived" from the value of the underlying stock.

Many investors, particularly those looking for a quick profit without making a careful analysis of the risks involved, have been "burned" by the explosion of derivative trading in the international markets. By the early 1990s, many investors—including California county funds, German trading companies, and British banks—had lost billions of dollars and even faced insolvency because they had bought derivatives, thinking that they would go up in value with little risk. When markets change direction, with interest rates rapidly falling or rising, for example, investors in derivatives can see their portfolio's value rise or fall precipitously.

Financial futures are among the most commonly traded derivatives, and often lead to enormous gains—and losses—for international investors. A future is simply an agreement to buy something for a fixed price at a certain future date. A financial future is an agreement to buy a financial instrument such as a stock or a bond. If the stock price goes up, or if interest rates move dramatically—affecting the price of the underlying bonds—a financial future can skyrocket or plummet precipitously.

Some financial futures are based on a whole range of instruments or on a complete market. A stock index future, for example, allows investors to benefit from the rise in a complete stock index, such as the Hang Seng Index in Hong Kong or the Standard & Poor's 500 in New York. Buying a stock index future is equivalent to buying all of the shares in the index. If the index goes up in value, the owner of the stock index future can profit handsomely. Just as a gold future goes up in value when gold's spot price rises, a Standard & Poor's 500 future—traded in Chicago—will increase in value when the stock index rises in New York.

Another commonly used derivative is a *swap*. The basic idea of any swap is to trade something you have for something you want. In the international financial markets, a swap is a trade agreement between two or more counterparties, usually banks, to exchange different assets or liabilities, such as interest payments.

Essentially, a swap allows both parties to obtain the right assets and cash flows for their own particular needs. In the case of banks, this most often means trading two loans with different interest rates or different currencies. A bank in France, for example, may be lending money to consumers in Paris at fixed interest rates. In order to fund these loans, the French bank may be borrowing U.S. dollars at floating—or periodically changing—interest rates. In order to eliminate the risk of having borrowed and lent money in two different currencies and at two different interest rates, the bank enters into a swap agreement with another institution. A bank in London or Mexico City may want to exchange their flow of interest rates with the French bank, so they enter into a swap agreement to each get what they want.

In theory, derivatives allow institutions and investors to get what they want—higher return, at a minimal risk. Because the world markets for derivatives have become so complex, most investors should follow the adage *caveat emptor*, or buyer beware. All investors, particularly those managing other people's money, should become aware of all of the risks involved before any venture into the exciting—and volatile—world of derivative trading.

42. WHAT IS AN OPTION?

IT IS ALWAYS worthwhile to keep our options open—to have the right but not the obligation to buy something at a guaranteed price in the future. In a time of fluctuating costs, for example, it is useful to have the option to buy a product at a guaranteed price. This allows us to take our time and shop around, knowing that we can always exercise our option to buy—if the price is right.

Since we use an option, or "exercise" it, only if it is profitable, it is always good to have as many options as we can. A racehorse owner with an option to buy a new thoroughbred at a certain price could use that option if the horse wins the Kentucky Derby. Or a sheep farmer in New Zealand could profit from having an option to sell wool at a guaranteed price at the end of each season, if the price of wool were to fall.

In the financial markets, where nothing of value is free, options cost money. The seller of the option has to be paid for taking the risk that the option will be exercised. The buyer of an option, on the other hand, will only use the option if it can make money—selling wool at a higher price than the current market, for example—so the buyer is willing to pay something for it. In general, the option holder's gain is the option seller's loss, and vice versa.

If the buyer of an option does not use the option during the allotted time, the buyer loses the money paid for it. If wool prices end up higher than the level guaranteed by a purchase option, for example, the New Zealand wool farmer will simply sell wool on the open market, letting the option expire unused.

There are many ways to value an option, but it really depends on the likelihood of its being used. An option that no one expects to exercise—or use—costs very little. However, an option will be quite expensive if there is a good chance it will be used. An option for a supply of umbrellas would be more expensive during a damp London winter than during a sweltering summer in Los Angeles.

Options can be created for anything that has uncertainty. No one knows for sure if a stock's price will go up or down, for example, so it is worthwhile to have an option to buy or sell that stock. If its price moves in the right direction, the holder of stock option can profit handsomely by exercising that option. An option's value essentially depends on the movement in value of the underlying asset, a stock or a commodity, for example.

Two other factors that influence an option's value are *volatility*, the amount of movement of the underlying asset's price, and *time value*, the amount of time for which the option is valid. An option based on an asset with high volatility, such as a stock with drastic swings in price, is worth more than one based on an asset that hardly ever changes in value. Likewise, an option that can be exercised for several years is more valuable than one that can be exercised for only a few months.

Investors need to be careful with options, because they are much more volatile than the underlying assets on which they are based. Because a stock option represents the right to buy or sell a large number of shares on the underlying stock, its price moves much more quickly—in both directions—than the stock price itself.

The world's first options were probably used in early agrarian societies, where options in the form of handshake agreements allowed farmers to hedge against the fluctuating prices of commodities such as wheat or grapes. In the expanding global economy, options and international options markets—from Chicago to Hong Kong—have grown to include a wide range of products, including foreign currency options, foreign stock options, and even options on other financial instruments, such as stock indexes, futures, and interest rates.

43. WHAT ARE PUTS AND CALLS?

THE INTERNATIONAL MARKETS are being increasingly driven by options trading, and investors in the global marketplace are offered a wide choice of options on everything from Sony stocks to Saudi crude oil and Singapore dollars. A Seattle coffee company, for example, may buy coffee options in São Paulo or New York to protect itself from unwanted market fluctuations, knowing that in the worst case it stands to lose only whatever it spent to buy the options in the first place.

Call options give the holder the right to buy, or "call in," something at a certain price and at a certain time in the future. *Put options* give the holder the right to sell, or put something into the option seller's hands, if it is not worth keeping.

The most popular options on the international markets are those that give the right to buy a certain number of shares, called the *underlying* shares, at a certain price during a limited period of time. Naturally, a call option goes up in value when the value of the underlying shares goes up.

On the other hand, stock "put" options give the right to sell shares at a fixed price. If the underlying stock's price goes down, making it worthwhile to sell at the put options price, put options will increase in value.

Who buys call options? Those who think the price of the underlying asset will go up. If the share prices go high enough, the holder of a call option can exercise the right to buy shares at a price lower than the market price. These shares can then be resold on the market for a profit. Alternately, the holder of a valuable call option can simply sell the option to someone else, at a profit, and avoid the trouble of exercising it.

Who buys put options? Those who think the price of the underlying asset will go down. If a share price drops low enough, the holder of a put option can exercise it by first buying shares in the market and then using the right to sell them at a higher price. The holder of a valuable put option can also sell the option to someone else, at a profit, to avoid the trouble of exercising it.

Call and put options give the investor a lot more bang for the buck. Instead of spending a lot of money to buy or sell the underlying assets, option investors can, for a relatively small amount of money invested, profit handsomely if the market moves in the right direction.

44. WHAT IS A CURRENCY OPTION?

ANYONE PLANNING A trip abroad or a business venture in another country would like to know what the foreign currency is going to be worth when the time comes to change money. Unwelcome currency fluctuations could make a shipment of grapes from Chile or a BMW import from Germany prohibitively expensive.

Currency options allow individual investors, businesses, or merchants to benefit from changes in the value of foreign currencies. By buying or selling currency options, it is possible to fix, in advance, exactly how many Swiss francs or Japanese yen a U.S. dollar can buy at a certain time in the future.

Just like other options, a currency option gives the holder the right, but not the obligation, to buy or sell something at a fixed price—in this case, a currency. The most common currency options are based on the U.S. dollar price of Swiss francs, French francs, German marks, British pounds, and Japanese yen.

Like all investments in the international marketplace, currency options can be used for speculation. Investors who believe that a currency will go up in value can buy an option and earn big money if they are right. If a currency goes up in value, the holder of an option to buy that currency—a currency "call" option—would profit. When the German mark rises, for example, its dollar value goes up and the holder of a German mark call option would benefit.

A currency option can also be used as a "hedge" by importers and exporters to guard against unwelcome changes in foreign currency values. A Texan anticipating buying a German automobile, for example, could buy German mark call options to "lock in" the U.S. dollar value of the import, thus avoiding any loss if the D-mark's value were to change before the automobile is purchased.

If a currency goes down in value, an option to sell it—a "put" option—would become more valuable. A Swiss franc put option, for example, which gives the holder the right to sell Swiss francs at a fixed price in the future, will be worth a lot if the Swiss franc declines in value on the international markets.

A Texas computer manufacturer anticipating sales to Switzerland could buy a Swiss franc put option to "lock in" the U.S. dollar value of the future sale, thus avoiding any loss if the value of the Swiss franc were to drop before the computers are sold in Zurich.

Exporters who earn money from all over the world economy often need to know what their bottom line will be in their own currency. Most companies, even small ones, use currency options to prevent earnings from being hurt by unwelcome currency fluctuations. With global trade now contributing to many companies' bottom lines, the use of currency options allows for the world economy to grow, unencumbered by the many different currencies used for international trade.

45. WHAT IS A WARRANT?

IN THE OLD WEST, a bounty hunter could seize a wanted outlaw by saying, "I have a warrant for your arrest!" A bounty hunter's warrant is similar to financial warrants in that it gives the holder certain rights. While frontier warrants gave the holder the right to arrest someone, most warrants in the world's financial markets give the holder the right to buy a company's shares.

Share purchase warrants, giving the holder the right to buy a company's shares at a certain price over a certain time, are different from normal stock options in that warrants are usually issued directly by the company, often in conjunction with a bond issue or a leveraged buyout.

Warrants can be attached to a bond, providing a "kicker" that gives investors an incentive to buy bonds with lower interest rates. Many Japanese companies, for example, have issued bonds with equity warrants attached, providing investors with an opportunity to buy the companies' shares. Like other options, warrants are used only when the price of the shares rises past their "striking price"—the price at which the shares can be purchased. When the market price of the shares shoots up, surpassing the warrant's striking price, the holder of the warrant profits by exercising the warrants or selling them to another investor.

Warrants are like coupons that can be removed from bonds and sold separately. Bonds traded with their warrants still attached are referred to as *cum*, the Latin for "with." Bonds without their warrants attached are referred to as *ex*, the Latin for "without."

As an alternative to warrants, a company may allow investors in certain bonds to "convert" the bonds into the company's stock. In contrast to an equity warrant giving investors the right to buy stocks with their own funds, a convertible bond gives the right to exchange the bond itself, at a fixed price and at a fixed time, into a certain number of the company's shares.

The purpose of warrants and convertible bonds is to offer investors a future reward—usually in the form of a company's shares—for accepting a lower interest on the company's bonds. Obviously, a country or international organization that does not have any shares would never be able to issue warrants or convertible bonds.

In the international markets, warrants are bought and sold in many different currencies, most notably Swiss francs, U.S. dollars, and Japanese yen. Many of the warrants traded on the New York Stock Exchange, for example, were issued in U.S. dollars by American companies looking for funds to finance mergers and acquisitions. Investors who buy these equity warrants are given the right to buy the merged company's shares at a point in the future, assuming they become more profitable.

The real value of a warrant is its time factor. When a company issues a warrant to buy its shares, it is providing a window of opportunity for investors to wait for the share prices to rise. The more time the investor has to exercise a warrant—providing more time for the share price to rise—the more valuable it is.

46. WHO INVESTS IN THE GLOBAL MARKETPLACE?

ANYONE INVESTING IN the international marketplace does so for one of three reasons: speculation, hedging, and arbitrage.

Most investors in the global markets are *speculators*. They believe that the market is heading in a certain direction, and they buy or sell in that belief. A Dutch pension fund buys shares on the Mexican stock exchange, for example, hoping to profit from an expected rise in the Mexican market. However, there is no way of knowing what will actually happen, and speculators never all agree on a particular direction or degree of movement in the international markets. Speculators take a risk. If the market moves in the right direction, they make a profit. If not, they lose.

The frenzied activity of speculators on the global markets is balanced by other players, hedgers and arbitragers, who seek precisely to avoid risk.

In contrast to speculators, for example, *hedgers* have no idea where prices will go. They want to protect themselves from a move in the wrong direction. For an elderly Canadian retiree, a logical hedge against unknown inflation would be to buy a house that would go up in value as the value of a fixed-income pension declined. Exporters also become hedgers when they buy currency options to guard against unknown changes in the value of their foreign currency earnings. The basic role of a hedger is to remove risk by making investments that balance the potential losses of other investments.

Arbitragers, on the other hand, try to take advantage of discrepancies in the market while avoiding risk. They buy in one market where something is cheap and sell it in another where the price is more expensive. A German tourist, for example, may be able to take advantage of price and currency differences by buying German-made compact disks in New York and selling them to friends at home. True arbitragers take no risk because they usually buy and sell at the same time, taking advantage of market inefficiencies. The term "arbitrager" is also sometimes used to describe takeover specialists who buy and sell under-valued companies.

Markets are usually made more efficient by the activities of speculators, hedgers, and arbitragers. For example, if the markets consisted only of hedgers, prices could rise and fall out of control. Speculators keep the market from becoming a one-way street by buying or selling whenever prices look attractive. Arbitragers, on the other hand, keep all of the world's markets in line by buying where the prices are too low and selling elsewhere, where prices have become too high.

47. WHAT IS HOT MONEY?

IT HAS BEEN said that a butterfly flapping its wings over Tokyo could cause a rain storm in New York's Central Park several days later. Events in the world economy are also interconnected—except that a change in the Tokyo markets can affect Wall Street, and other markets around the world, almost instantaneously.

When the New York stock markets dropped precipitously in 1987, for example, markets around the world immediately followed suit. When England's Baring's Bank was on the brink of collapse at the beginning of 1995, central banks from London to Singapore moved quickly to avoid a financial meltdown. And when Mexico's economy faltered in 1994 and the peso plunged, investors from around the world pulled billions of dollars worth of "hot money" out of Latin American markets in a matter of days, pushing several countries to the brink of financial ruin.

Hot money, also called "smart money," consists of the hundreds of billions of dollars of funds that can come flowing in and out of an economy at a moment's notice. Since hot money managers are usually the first to react to any news in the global economy, currencies and bond markets around the world can decline—or rise—precipitously, as hot money gets transferred with the velocity of electronic transfers.

Although hot money is usually managed by big banks or investment groups, it actually represents the savings and investments of millions of people throughout the world. It comes from almost every country and is made up of almost every currency. Hot money ranges from New York banks investing pension fund dollars in Indonesia to New Delhi corporations investing rupees in Canada.

The "information age" has brought the world together in ways never imagined when the first live television coverage was broadcast from the Tokyo Olympics of 1964. Now, with a plethora of international news services beaming information into bank trading floors and airport lounges from Johannesburg to Jamaica, investors are immediately informed of any changes in the world economy.

The world economy's investor base has also been changing. With electronic pagers and home computers guiding them through the maze of financial information, individuals from around the world are taking an increasingly active role in investing their savings. When these investments are grouped into funds, the volume is astounding. For example, the California Public Employees Retirement Fund, one of the world's biggest investors, has literally billions of dollars to be invested at any given time.

When a fund manager sees a television report indicating a country's impending decline, a decision can be taken immediately to remove funds from that country's economy. An astute fund manager on vacation in Hawaii, for example, may see a television report that the Mexican peso is about to fall and decide to sell all funds invested in Latin America. A simple call can set in motion a chain of events felt even in the smallest village in Argentina.

By giving an order to redeem $500,000 of an emerging market equity fund, for example, a solitary investor soon has money flowing from one world financial center to another. The emerging market fund sold on a London Exchange, for example, may hold shares in several Argentine companies. When the order comes in to redeem shares in the fund, the managers immediately sell the shares in Argentina to reduce the fund's investments. The "sell" order coming from London immediately appears on the Buenos Aires stock exchange, and the company's shares may consequently decline in value. Other investors may want to "get on the bandwagon"—or, in this case, sell the company's shares. The company is forced to react, possibly by laying off workers in a small town in Patagonia.

The money pulled out of Argentina may end up, on the same day, in completely different parts of the world economy: invested in a Dutch electronics company, for example, or an Indonesian mutual fund, or in a U.S. government bond. With a few simple transactions, banks and trading houses around the world move money into—and out of—economies, with only a moment's notice.

As the scale of these transfers increases, disaster can result. It is estimated that more than a trillion dollars of hot money is moving around the world at any given time. This money, more than the total annual economic output of most countries, can move into an economy in one day—following favorable economic news, for example—and be pulled out at a moment's notice if the currency falls in value or other signs point to an economic slowdown.

For comparison's sake, the value of all of the world's gold mined since King Solomon's day is estimated to be only a fraction of the value of investments in the world's derivatives markets on any given day. Like all financial investors, the owners of this speculative flood of hot money are simply looking for a favorable return on their investment. Essentially, they are looking for countries that have sound financial policies and reasonable prospects for growth—and profits.

Some world leaders have called for the imposition of a tax on the speculative flows of hot money, arguing that the unbridled flows of capital around the world are responsible for political and social upheaval. Some have even called for the imposition of a tax—called the "Tobin tax" after the Nobel Prize–winning economist who first proposed it—that would be applied to global capital flows and provide money for "social" investment in the Third World.

There is no guarantee, however, that such funds would actually be used properly in the countries of the developing world. It could be that the access to unlimited global capital would do more good for the developing countries than handouts from rich countries or banks.

In fact, the discipline of the international capital markets can be quite beneficial, by forcing governments to make politically difficult decisions, and to cut government spending, if they want to continue to attract foreign investment. Those economies that succeed in attracting international funds can benefit enormously. The billions of dollars of funds invested in the emerging markets during the early 1990s, for example, fueled economic growth around the world, creating many jobs, financing infrastructure, and paving the way for much-needed political and economic reform.

48. HOW DO INVESTORS AND BUSINESSES USE INFORMATION TECHNOLOGY TO ACCESS THE GLOBAL ECONOMY?

THE INFORMATION SUPERHIGHWAY, often referred to internationally as the "Infobahn," has revolutionized international business and international investing. Where investors once relied on reading a newspaper to get day-old financial information, and where business once used letters sent by ships and airplanes to communicate with overseas clients, communication now occurs in a split second.

With access to satellite television news and a cellular telephone, a major fund manager sitting on a small Caribbean island can be as well informed of major events as someone sitting on Wall Street or in downtown Tokyo. Computers now allow businesses and investors to receive and analyze a plethora of digitalized information, permitting them to participate in the world economy in ways unheard of less than a decade before.

One of the major tools used by businesses and investors in the world economy is on-line information. By the mid-1990s there were more than one hundred information services providing global stock quotations and other financial data to investors with on-line computers. Investors from Boston to Bangkok now have the capability to scan thousands of stocks and investment funds for information on dividends, earnings, and growth forecasts, in virtually every market on the globe.

The first tool any investor or business needs to succeed in the world economy is knowledge of the economic environment. An average investor can wake up to a vast array of news sources, ranging from a twenty-four-hour satellite news program to the latest financial reports on a local business radio station. In addition, information from all of the major news organizations can now be accessed at home on a home computer or on Videotext services. Almost all European television channels, for example, have Videotext pages provided free to all viewers equipped with a decoder. Any political or market change can be instantly detected and researched by scanning the thousands of pages of free information.

But news is not the only necessary ingredient for good investment decisions. Basic data needs to be easily accessed to allow any investor, whether an Iowa farmer or a Scottish fund manager, to understand the global markets. Home computers, for example, can now be linked to a wide range of services providing information on stocks, bonds, derivatives, and historical price information.

Investors on the move can also use personal digital assistants (PDAs), which not only tell the price of almost any type of investment, including gold, stocks, and currencies, but also allow the investor to communicate with a broker or bank to give instructions on which instruments to buy or sell at any given time. These "wireless" hand-held devices have little screens that can show the latest quotes for your favorite stock, option, or hog belly future price.

During the period of hyperinflation in Brazil, for example, an innovative bank provided all of its important customers with a small digital device that provided the latest prices of gold and inflation-linked financial instruments. These hand-held devices often use a combination of several different technologies: PDAs can function as a combination computer, telephone, fax, and pager. With a global satellite system in place, these portable devices will be able to send and receive information anywhere on the face of the earth.

The basic component of most technology in the global information infrastructure can be summed up in one word: digital. By moving away from sound waves that transmit traditional "analog" information, the information superhighway is being built with technology that breaks down all information into small bits that can be read and stored by any computer. The advantage of the digital revolution is that information can now be stored and manipulated by any investor or business in the world economy.

Most on-line services also provide stock and bond quotations, with short delays. Those that show quotes in "real time" usually have to pay a fee, to the New York Stock Exchange, for example, which is passed on to the subscriber. While some concentrate on providing data, others provide research and timely news, such as new issues and dividends. Basically, the system operator decides what information is provided and what is not. Some do not provide historical prices; others provide only a limited amount of stocks and bonds. All of this digitalized information can help investors tell if a particular investment is undervalued, overvalued, or fairly valued.

Information technology has opened up a whole world of investing to individuals and funds. By the 1990s, the U.S. share of the global economy, and the value of its stock and bond markets, had declined to approximately one third of the world total. Any responsible investor, therefore, is increasingly required to look to the global economy for a diversified portfolio of investments.

To access the expanding global economy, many investors and businesses are also turning to the World Wide Web, which has expanded to allow businesses to market their goods and services in every corner of the world. A computer in Boston can access the "Web" for the same cost—usually a local telephone call—as a French investor using an on-line "Minitel" terminal or a Thai business manager using a personal digital assistant in Bangkok. Business in cyberspace can often be just as lucrative as that in a local shopping center. The advantage is that the customer base now encompasses the whole world.

49. WHAT ARE THE FORCES BEHIND EUROPEAN ECONOMIC UNITY?

UNITING A CONTINENT with more than forty countries and almost as many languages, currencies, cultures, and political systems is not an easy task. Apart from brief periods of pan-European military rule—such as the Roman or the Napoleonic empires—Europe has been divided by sturdy political and ethnic barriers that have defied many attempts at unification. England, for example, has often preferred to maintain closer relations with its former colonies around the world than with its European neighbors. Other countries, such as Switzerland, have sought to preserve their independence and neutrality at all costs.

By the beginning of the 1990s, however, the continent of Europe found itself completely transformed by political and economic upheaval. The fall of the Soviet bloc, which had divided the continent for over four decades, brought a completely new economic order.

The quest for European unity has involved three distinct groups of countries: the members of the European Union (EU), the Western European countries that refused to join the EU, and the formerly communist countries of Eastern Europe eager to join the capitalist West. Uniting these nations would produce the most powerful economic bloc in the world. With a population and economy exceeding that of China, Japan, or the United States, an integrated Europe would be a true economic super-power.

Uniting Europe, however, has proven to be a nearly im-possible task. Some wealthy countries in Western Europe re-fused to join the major European economies in their free-trade "club," the European Union. Switzerland, for example, with one of the highest per capita incomes in the world and a long history of neutrality, in the early 1990s refused the proposal to integrate into the European Union.

Previously, several of Europe's wealthiest economies had formed a separate trade association called EFTA (the European Free Trade Association), which originally included seven of the richest European countries: Austria, Finland, Iceland, Liechtenstein, Norway, Sweden, and Switzerland. By the early 1990s, the European Union proposed forming with the EFTA countries a common economic trading zone, called the Euro-pean Economic Area (EEA). When Switzerland refused to join, Liechtenstein felt obliged to stay out, as well. Neighboring Aus-tria, however, applied for full EU membership and joined in 1995.

In Scandinavia, Finland and Sweden also decided to join the European Union in 1995. Norway, however, refused to join, citing their strong economic position, as well as a long-standing fear of losing political independence to the larger European countries. Countries such as Norway, Switzerland, Liech-tenstein, and Iceland decided to try to develop special trade agreements that would allow them to have access to the EU market while maintaining their neutrality and political independence.

The Eastern European countries, finding the doors for full EU membership temporarily locked, requested special trade conditions. The EU actively promoted this idea of economic enfranchisement, which would allow the other countries in Europe to trade with the EU, without granting them full membership. In this way, instead of being left out in the cold, the non-EU countries could keep doing business with the rest of Europe without overloading the EU with too many new members.

50. WHAT IS THE EUROPEAN UNION?

FRENCH PRESIDENT Charles de Gaulle used to complain that it was impossible to govern a country that produced 385 different cheeses. Imagine, then, joining France to several other European countries to form a common market of many different languages, cultures, bureaucracies, and legal systems. The European Union (EU) has succeeded, however, in joining together a group of countries in an economic and political union that has come close to achieving the age-old dream of a "United States" of Europe.

The EU had its beginning in 1957 when six countries—Belgium, France, the Netherlands, Italy, Luxembourg, and West Germany—signed the Treaty of Rome to form the European Coal and Steel Community, later called the European Economic Community (EEC). Originally, the EEC was intended to be a customs union, removing tariffs and quotas on trade among its member countries.

As the EEC grew during the 1970s and 1980s to include Britain, Ireland, Denmark, Greece, Spain, and Portugal, it became known as the European Community or EC. The original treaties were expanded by a variety of political, agricultural, industrial, and monetary agreements, including the Common Agricultural Policy (CAP) that guaranteed large subsidies to European farmers.

To simplify the bookkeeping, the European Currency Unit (ECU) was created, with an official value based on a "basket" of currencies. The idea was to have a central common unit of accounts that would be more stable than any one of the currencies making up the ECU. Subsequently, it became a popular currency in its own right, with "ECU" bank accounts, bonds, and checking accounts.

Eventually, the member states of the European Community decided to consolidate into an economic and political union similar to the United States or Canada. They decided that the best way to encourage trade and economic growth was to remove all barriers, economic or otherwise, between member countries. The plan, named after the Dutch town where it was signed, Maastricht, came to symbolize this drive for a revitalized Europe.

By removing all internal barriers, the newly named European Union (EU) hoped to create a truly common market that would enjoy all the advantages of standardized regulations, industries, financial systems, transportation, communications, and taxes. Citizens in Portugal could move to London or Amsterdam to work without any extra paperwork; goods could flow from Holland to Italy without barriers; and money could be transferred from Madrid to Frankfurt without delays.

In 1995, three new members—Austria, Finland, and Swe-

den—brought the total of EU countries to 15. In accepting inte-
gration, the countries of the European Union agreed to surren-
der a part of their national sovereignty in order to achieve
something they perceived to be of far greater value: economic
and political strength.

51. HOW DO COMMUNIST COUNTRIES PARTICIPATE IN THE WORLD ECONOMY?

FROM CHINA AND Cuba to Vietnam and North Korea,
communist countries have not only participated in the world
economy, they have often prospered enormously in their "capitalist" enterprises.

In the early 1990s, for example, the People's Republic of
China, was able to sustain economic growth that rivaled any
country in the capitalist world. Much of this growth was based
on exports to the same capitalist countries that had once threatened war to make China change its "communist" ways.

The communist system was based on an economic and social theory, developed by Karl Marx in the nineteenth century,
that called for a takeover of the state by the workers. This "dic-
tatorship of the proletariat" would, he thought, pave the way to
true socialism. The goal was to replace the pain and inequities of
capitalism with "communism," an economic system where life is
organized on the principle "from each according to his abilities,
to each according to his needs."

While it has been used for a wide variety of political purposes, communism is an economic system that was meant to provide an alternative to the perceived excesses of unbridled capitalism. Instead of letting the markets make the major economic decisions, a communist economy puts decision-making power into the hands of the central government, in the hopes of creating a more egalitarian "communal" society.

Although communist central planning has brought about strong economic growth in some countries—such as China in the 1990s and the Soviet Union of the 1920s and 1930s—it has often resulted in long-term inefficiency and economic stagnation. Central planners often concentrate on maintaining industrial dinosaurs, such as steel plants or shipyards, that employ millions of people but often produce products of inferior quality and rampant pollution.

After World War II, for example, the communist countries of Eastern Europe saw their modest postwar growth outstripped by the dazzling wealth and power of their capitalist neighbors to the West. For decades, one only needed to look at divided Berlin—rich and gushing with confidence in the West, gray and crumbling in the East—to understand the disadvantages of communism.

With the collapse of the Soviet Union, the remaining communist economies, such as Cuba and Vietnam, were forced in the early 1990s to attempt a new form of communism—one with a distinctly capitalist face. The lack of foreign funds, for example, forced Cuba to adopt a parallel "dollar" economy that saw the wealth accumulate in the hands of those who had access to foreign currency. The poor underclass with the almost worthless "pesos normales" were not allowed to eat in restaurants frequented by those with access to dollars. Paradoxically, this division of economic classes is precisely what communism was supposed to abolish.

The new Cuban economy, although still providing universal health care and education, was forced by economic constraints to drastically alter its communist path. By moving toward an economy that rewarded citizens earning foreign currency and allowing foreign companies to buy parts of the Cuban economy, Cuban communism had begun to clearly resemble its capitalist neighbors to the north and south.

China's communist leaders, after enjoying nearly a decade of double-digit economic growth, were also confronted with a dilemma in the early 1990s: how to continue providing the economic freedom that allowed the provinces to grow even further, while retaining central political control.

The debate in China, as in many other Asian countries with autocratic governments, centered on how much the people could be allowed to do economically, without opening the doors to political freedom. Democracy, one of the main demands of the students killed by government troops in Tiananmen Square in 1989, is often the first request from people who have been given a taste of economic freedom.

52. HOW DID THE SOCIALIST COUNTRIES OF THE SOVIET BLOC MAKE THE TRANSITION TO CAPITALISM?

W HEN THE SOCIALIST countries of the former Soviet Union and Eastern Europe retreated from communism at the end of the 1980s, their "worst-case" scenario began with economics, not politics.

One of their worst fears, as they made the difficult economic transition from communism to capitalism, was that they could easily lose their newly won political freedom. This fear was quickly reinforced by the failed old-guard coup in the Soviet Union and by later revolts in several former Soviet Republics and autonomous regions, such as Azerbaijan and Chechnya.

When most of the Eastern European countries transformed their economies in the early 1990s, jettisoning state industries and opening the doors to capitalism, a heady period of euphoria followed. Western bankers rushed to open offices in Prague, Budapest, and Kiev. People from the Danube to the Urals saw the end of totalitarianism as the beginning of a new golden age of economic prosperity.

But the fruits of capitalism are seldom enjoyed immediately. The eagerly awaited prosperity of the free-market systems in Eastern Europe would be a long time coming. In their drive to privatize state industries and remove restrictions on ownership and investments, many Eastern European countries experienced painful economic recession.

Their transition from communism to capitalism was often hindered by a crumbling infrastructure and rising unemployment, leading to hyperinflation and political unrest. Since most workers had lived all of their lives under totalitarianism, they were unable to understand even the basics of capitalism and democracy. Workers in Eastern Europe became reluctant to give up guaranteed jobs and social welfare for the elusive promise of capitalist economic growth.

As a result, some countries in Eastern Europe opted for a hybrid economic system. During an interim period, the government would provide an economic safety net while moving forward slowly to reform the economy. This combination of socialism and capitalism was inspired by the economic system of Western countries such as Sweden and France, which had been relatively successful in combining the advantages of socialism with the dynamism of the free market.

Other countries opted to go all the way and make an immediate transition to capitalism. The Federal Republic of Germany's decision to quickly transform East Germany into a fully functioning capitalist economy was a prime example. Huge investments in infrastructure such as highways and telephone systems and in the restructuring of inefficient industries put an enormous drain on the resources of one of the world's richest countries. Even with hundreds of billions of German marks pouring into the economy, the former East Germany took many years to even begin to resemble a successful capitalist economy.

Further east, countries such as Russia and the Baltic republics of Latvia, Lithuania, and Estonia also moved quickly to dismantle the communist apparatus. The goal was to quickly transform the economy—and its society—before reactionary forces had a chance to force a return to authoritarian rule. Privatization of formerly state-run industries was undertaken at a rapid pace.

Although they risked popular discontent and many years

of economic austerity, most countries found that the only way to overcome decades of economic mismanagement was a complete transition to a free-market economy, with currency convertibility and no price controls. Under this capitalist system, the people and the markets were to be allowed to make all of the decisions, no matter how painful.

53. WHAT IS THE PACIFIC RIM ECONOMY?

OVER THE PAST three thousand years, the world has changed its economic center of activity several times. Once, the world economy was based in the Mediterranean, where Egypt, Greece, and Rome founded their prosperous economies on seafaring trade. At other times, international trade and commerce made parts of China, India, and the Middle East centers of vast wealth and power.

With European expansion into the Western Hemisphere, following Columbus's voyage of 1492—and with the rise of the great trading nations of England, Holland, Spain, and Portugal—the Atlantic became the new center for international trade and commerce. This continued throughout the Industrial Revolution, as the United States and its major trading partners in northern Europe built the world's most advanced and wealthiest nations on the Atlantic's edge.

With the dramatic rise of Japan and other Asian and Pacific economies after World War II, however, the world began to turn its attention to the Pacific. The United States, Canada,

Mexico, Chile, Australia, New Zealand, South Korea, Hong Kong, Thailand, Singapore, China, and Japan, which are all located on the Pacific Rim, have become major trading nations. By the early 1990s, the trade between these economies constituted almost half of the world's total.

The rapid economic growth of many Pacific Rim countries, particularly Japan, was based essentially on exports. By efficiently producing large amounts of consumer goods, these countries succeeded in building up enormous trade surpluses. South Korea, for example, based its economic growth on exports of consumer goods such as televisions and VCRs that would end up in homes in Europe and North America.

The elite club of Pacific Rim powerhouses has gradually expanded to include groups such as Asia's "Four Tigers": South Korea, Singapore, Taiwan, and Hong Kong. Once backward, low-income countries, these "Four Tigers" had made such rapid economic progress during the 1970s and 1980s that they were included in the select group of advanced Third World countries called Newly Industrialized Countries (NICs).

Another grouping of the rapidly growing Southeast Asian countries is called ASEAN, or Association of South East Asian Nations. This economic and political alliance—consisting of Brunei, Indonesia, Malaysia, the Philippines, Singapore, and Thailand—was set up to encourage trade and economic growth among its members. Indeed, the economic growth rates of several ASEAN countries, Thailand and Malaysia in particular, have been among the highest in the world.

Realizing that their economies have a long way to go to catch up with industrial giants in North America and Europe, many rapidly growing countries in the Pacific Rim have made efforts to remove trade barriers. Just as the nations of Europe formed the Common Market to stimulate economic growth, the

Newly Industrialized Countries of the Pacific Rim have turned to regional trade alliances in order to share in the political and economic advantages of expanded international trade.

54. WHAT IS JAPAN INC.?

THE EXTRAORDINARY SUCCESS of Japan's postwar economy can be traced in part to the alliance of its government and private sector. This giant national enterprise, often called "Japan Inc.," is based on the mercantilist policy of encouraging exports while avoiding importing goods and services from abroad. Like any new kid on the block, Japan's success in building up large trade surpluses has angered many of its trading partners.

The success of the Japanese export machine results largely from a strictly controlled national effort led by the Japanese Ministry for International Trade and Industry (MITI). Some competitors say that the Japanese export machine has worked too well, taking advantage of the global system of free trade while keeping a complex set of trade barriers at home. Many Japanese leaders say that the rest of the world buys Japanese products simply because they are better made and are sold at competitive prices, using the age-old argument, "Build a better mousetrap, and the world will beat a path to your door."

Indeed, the high quality of many Japanese products is responsible in large part for their success on the world markets. This success can be partly explained by the long-term view that

most Japanese companies have taken in developing and manufacturing new products. Many of Japan's competitors in other
parts of the world have been criticized for concentrating on
short-term profits and failing to pursue the long-term research
and development necessary to bring competitive products to
Japanese markets.

Foreign products marketed in Japan, however, often en-
counter hidden cultural barriers. For example, many Japanese
consumers are simply wary of foreign products and their perceived inferior quality. There are also layers of protectionism
stemming from the Japanese practice of cross-ownership of
much of its industry, called *keiretsu*, in which a company will
buy products from other companies in its group instead of importing cheaper goods from abroad.

Upon close scrutiny, however, most trade surpluses can be
traced to efficiency and hard work. As long as countries have
different laws, certain barriers will always exist. But instead of
putting up trade barriers or "bashing" countries in the world
economy, it is usually more productive to cooperate with all of
the players to create a truly level playing field, open to every
country in the world.

55. WHAT IS NAFTA?

THE NORTH AMERICAN Free Trade Agreement, created in 1988, originally encompassed only the economies of the United States and Canada. NAFTA's goal was simple: to remove barriers to trade.

Later, when Mexico was added as a member, NAFTA was able to combine several diverse countries with a classic system of division of labor allowing each country to do what it does best—earning precious foreign reserves from its exports and using the money to pay for increased imports.

The advantages of free trade are seldom more apparent than in countries with vastly different climates and economic infrastructures. The Americans and Canadians who founded NAFTA saw that a free-trade area in North America, stretching from the cold Arctic tundra to balmy Caribbean shores, would be essential if the countries were to take advantage of each other's strengths. Instead of wasting precious labor and resources trying to grow bananas or tobacco in the cold Yukon, for example, Canadians could be much better off importing these goods from their warmer neighbors to the south.

Conversely, the Mexicans who joined NAFTA saw that it would be much cheaper to allow Wal-mart to come in and sell well-made American products, making Mexico's economy more efficient and allowing it to be a more successful exporter to other countries in the world economy.

In the United States and Canada, the debate over NAFTA

centered mainly on jobs. How could each country open its borders to trade, and a flood of better-made and cheaper imports, without losing jobs? The leaders of the NAFTA countries realized that closing borders to trade would, in the long term, lead to a loss of competitiveness and an eventual loss of jobs for a nation that lost its ability to compete on the world markets. They realized that the world economy is not a zero-sum game, where one country's gain was another country's loss. Open markets, in the long term, would provide the incentive for producers on both sides of the border to concentrate on producing only those goods and services in which they had a competitive advantage. In addition, the constant pressure from foreign competitors would force each country to improve the quality and value of its products.

Canada, for example, saw that in importing manufactured appliances from Mexico or aircraft from the United States, Canada's economy would be better off by making it more efficient. They also realized that this logic would only hold if Canadians had the freedom to export goods and services to the United States and Mexico. By exporting products at which they hold a competitive advantage, such as timber, banking services, sporting goods, and maple syrup, Canadians could earn foreign exchange. These earnings could then be used to import those goods and services, ranging from bananas to computer software, produced more efficiently by its neighbors to the south.

NAFTA is strictly a free-trade agreement. It simply calls for the complete removal of barriers to trade between the member countries. Unlike the European Union's structure, which put up common trade barriers to countries outside their economic "fortress," NAFTA limited itself to removing internal trade barriers. NAFTA also made no attempt to adopt a common market policy allowing free movement of people from one member country to another.

Although much of the trade in North America was already tariff-free, the pact reinforced free-market reforms and further stimulated cross-border economic activity. Instead of taking jobs away from workers in the United States and Canada, it was shown that a growing Mexican economy would not only provide more jobs for its people at home, reducing immigration northward, but would also provide a growing market for goods and services from the United States and Canada.

Despite the economic crisis experienced by Mexico in the mid-1990s, NAFTA's success was clearly demonstrated by an initial increase in jobs and economic growth, on both sides of the border. During the first year of trading with Mexico, for example, the United States saw a surge of exports, ranging from semiconductors to apples, and the Mexican economy boomed. Canada, Mexico, and the United States, inspired by the initial success of free trade in North America, then moved to allow other countries from the Western Hemisphere, such as Chile, to join in NAFTA's expanding free-trade zone.

56. WHAT ARE FREE-TRADE MEGAZONES?

INSPIRED BY THE success of the free-trade zones in Europe and in North America, in the early 1990s most players in the global economy moved to build alliances based on the principle that lowering barriers to trade means increased economic activity for everyone.

By the mid-1990s, several free-trade "megazones" had

begun to form. Unlimited access to world markets was seen as beneficial not only for consumers, but also to businesses—especially the efficient ones. Exports from the United States, for example, ranging from Seattle aircraft to Midwest grain and New York financial services, provided an enormous boost to the domestic economy and created hundreds of thousands of new jobs.

By opening up borders to trade, rich countries in North America and Western Europe are also able to stimulate growth in the developing countries of the Third World. By importing cheaper goods from developing countries, the industrialized countries provide their own consumers with a wider range of products. These imports also stimulate the growth of jobs and markets abroad, many of which are desperately in need of an economic "jump start." In turn, economic growth in the developing countries expands the market for industrialized countries' goods and services, ranging from German cars to Hollywood movies, leading to more growth, and more jobs, worldwide.

One of the world's most successful free-trade "megazones" could already be found in Europe. After successfully integrating the economies of Sweden, Austria, and Finland in the mid-1990s, the European Union began to prepare to expand eastward. By incorporating the healthiest economies of Eastern Europe—Poland, the Czech Republic, Slovakia, Hungary, and the Baltic republics of Lithuania, Latvia, and Estonia—the European Common Market would extend its reach from the Atlantic to the western border of Russia. This European free-trade megazone could eventually encompass one of the world's richest conglomerations of industrial economies.

In addition, further expansion of the European megazone would follow the lead of the "Latin" EU members, Italy, Spain, and Portugal, and expand further into the Mediterranean. By opening up its borders to trade with Northern Africa, Cyprus,

Turkey, and eventually including Israel and the Arab countries of the Middle East, the European Union could include a vast array of economies, cultures, and political systems. The goal of this expansion into a Euro-Mediterranean free-trade megazone would be to foster not only economic growth, but also political stability—in hopes of guaranteeing peaceful and secure borders for its member states.

Faced with these plans to create an economic megazone in Europe, the leaders of the Western Hemisphere also began to prepare for a free-trade zone stretching from the Arctic to the Antarctic. At a summit meeting in Miami in 1994, plans were announced to create a "Free Trade Area of the Americas" including all of the capitalist economies of North, Central, and South America.

As a first step to a free-trade megazone in the Americas, several free-trade zones had been set up by the mid-1990s. Besides NAFTA, with its three trading partners in North America, free-trade zones had been established throughout Central and South America. Mercosur (Mercado Commún del Sur, or in Brazil: Mercosul—Mercado Comum do Sul), joined Argentina, Brazil, Uruguay, and Paraguay, and opened up Brazil's gigantic economy to its Southern Cone neighbors for the first time. By the mid-1990s Brazil's exports to Argentina had tripled, with Brazilian beer, automobiles, and banking services flooding southward. The region's healthiest economy, Chile, while waiting for admission to NAFTA, was content to take a back seat in opening up trade within the Southern Cone.

Further to the north, the Andean Pact also removed internal barriers to trade among the five economies of Venezuela, Columbia, Peru, Ecuador, and Bolivia. The total size of these South American economic blocs was only a fraction of NAFTA, with the United States economy being much larger than all of its neighbors in the Americas, but it was hoped that these smaller blocs would stimulate economic growth throughout the region.

The other, smaller countries of Central and South America also joined to form two trading blocks: the Central American Common Market—including Guatemala, Costa Rica, El Salvador, Honduras, and Nicaragua; and the Caribbean Community (CARICOM) free-trade zone—including Jamaica, Trinidad & Tobago, and Surinam.

These two smaller free-trade zones, as well as the European Union, had one major free-trade drawback: they all built Common External Tariffs (CETs) to discourage imports from outside their zones. The idea of these CETs was to allow the economies to develop sufficiently, without competition from cheaper foreign products. It was assumed that later, with economies able to withstand competition from abroad, these external tariffs would be removed.

NAFTA, with its eye on the future Free Trade Area of the Americas, moved to prohibit the imposition of any barriers to trade, even those on products from outside the trade zone. The NAFTA example, to be applied to the Western Hemisphere economic megazone, would lead to the complete removal of trade barriers such as tariffs, even those that applied to products from outside the trading zone.

The colossal size of the Asian economies has also led to the formation of a free-trade megazone centered on the Pacific Rim. The proposed "Asia-Pacific Free Trade Area," presented at a meeting of the eighteen-country Asia-Pacific Economic Cooperation Forum, in Indonesia in 1994, would incorporate most of the world's largest economies. In addition to the two largest economies in the world, Japan and the United States, the Pacific Rim megazone would include China, which was expected to become one of the world's biggest economic powerhouses by the twenty-first century. With almost half the world's population, and almost half the world's output and trade, the Pacific megazone would by far surpass the size of the other free-trade areas of the global economy.

The idea was to eventually merge these large trading groups. The possibility of linking the North American Free Trade Area to the Asia-Pacific Free Trade Area was already discussed at the formation of the Asia Pacific free-trade megazone in 1994. In theory, with the GATT agreements and the World Trade Organization leading the way, the free-trade zones of the future would combine to form one, barrier-free, world economy.

57. WHAT IS THE THIRD WORLD?

THE TERM *THIRD WORLD* was originally devised to describe the poor and developing countries of the world economy. It was based on the idea that the "first" and "second" worlds were made up of the free-market and centrally planned countries with advanced industrial economies. This "developed" world was seen to include most of the countries of Eastern and Western Europe, as well as the United States, Canada, Australia, New Zealand, and Japan.

The countries of the Third World can be divided into three groups: those developing rapidly, those developing moderately, and the poorest few, whose economies are not developing at all.

At the top of the list of Third World nations are the rapidly developing countries called Newly Industrialized Countries

(NICs). Most lists of NICs include Brazil, Argentina, Hong Kong, Israel, Mexico, Singapore, South Africa, South Korea, and Taiwan.

These "lucky few" are seen to be on their way to joining the ranks of the advanced economies of the world.

The bulk of the Third World consists of a large group of moderately developing economies that includes most of the countries in Africa, Asia, and Latin America. The most populous countries in this group are India, China, Indonesia, and Malaysia, which together comprise more than half of the world's population.

At the bottom of the list are the world's poorest countries, found mainly in sub-Sahara Africa, which have so few resources and so little money that it is virtually impossible for them to develop at all. In Somalia and Sudan, for example, there are essentially no natural resources on which to base economic growth. This group is sometimes called the "Fourth World."

Although the Third World comprises three quarters of the world's population and 90 percent of the world's population growth, it provides only 20 percent of the world's economic production. And although the Third World holds much of the world's natural resources—including vast petroleum reserves in Latin America, Asia, and the Middle East—much of the raw materials from the Third World are shipped abroad for consumption by the world's wealthier and more developed countries.

58. WHAT ARE THE ROOTS OF THIRD WORLD POVERTY?

ECONOMIC AND POLITICAL misjudgment can be blamed for much of the Third World's poverty, but an important factor has also been the population explosion. Many developing countries have seen their populations double in as little as twenty years. This growth was due mainly to lack of birth control and declining mortality rates, resulting from improved medical care.

Extreme poverty in the Third World has forced many parents to create ever larger families, hoping that their children can work and increase family income. But the economic opportunities are often not available, and unemployed children and their parents end up moving into already overcrowded cities, in a fruitless search for work.

Many underdeveloped nations have found themselves in a vicious circle of poverty and overpopulation, with no hope in sight. The flood of poor families into major cities puts enormous strain on the economic infrastructure. Shantytowns in such cities as Bombay, São Paulo, and Shanghai have become glaring reminders that the world economy has left behind many of the world's poor.

Saddled with enormous debt payments, hyperinflation, surging populations, and mounting unemployment, many Third World countries struggle just to keep their economies afloat. Sometimes, with no money available for investment, even the infrastructure, such as roads and water systems, literally falls apart.

The solution for many overburdened governments is to simply increase debt in order to keep the money flowing. However, this often results in rampant inflation, which ends up eroding most of these efforts, and creates an ever-widening gap between the Third World's poorest and richest economies.

59. WHAT ARE THE ORIGINS OF THE THIRD WORLD'S DEBT?

DURING THE OIL booms of the 1970s, the oil-rich Arab countries of the Middle East turned to the world's major banks, primarily in the United States and Europe, to provide a safe home for their newly earned petrodollars. These interest-bearing deposits, sitting in the coffers of Western banks, needed to be recycled—lent out to interest-paying borrowers—in order for the banks to earn money.

Many banks with these large deposits of petrodollars chose to make enormous loans to the Third World. These loans were used, in part, to pay for those countries' ever-increasing oil imports. This game of revolving cash would have disastrous consequences for many developing economies.

At the time, loans with floating interest rates looked irresistible to governments keen on developing their economies: indeed, the interest rates were so low they were not even keeping up with inflation in many of the countries. Borrowing money looked like a no-lose proposition. In this way, countries with strong growth rates, such as Mexico and Brazil, were able to borrow tens of billions of dollars at bargain-basement prices.

The goal of the debtor governments was to borrow as much as possible in a gamble: by borrowing cheap money, they hoped to build new infrastructure and new industries that would produce enough exports to pay back the loans in the future.

Brazil, for example, during the 1960s and 1970s, had one of the highest growth rates in the world. Its economy was producing an ever-increasing surplus of food, clothing, and manufactured goods. It had grown from a poor, underdeveloped nation to become the world's eighth largest economy. Brazil looked as though it had worked an economic miracle. Then interest rates skyrocketed and the steep rise in oil prices forced the country to borrow heavily to pay for increased oil imports, and economic mismanagement eventually led to gyrating inflation rates and economic stagnation.

Not only were many debtor countries unable to pay back the principal—the original amount borrowed—often they were not even able to keep up with the interest payments. Only by rescheduling these loans, in effect admitting that they could not be paid back immediately, could the banks begin to come to terms with the enormous problems of the Third World debt.

Although part of the Third World debt was borrowed from governments and international agencies like the World Bank and the International Monetary Fund, the greatest portion was borrowed from banks in North America, Japan, and Western Europe. Those borrowing the money were primarily Third World governments. Not all Third World debt was in U.S. dollars, however. Many loans were made in other currencies, such as German marks and British pounds, but they are all usually translated into dollars to make the debt figures easier to understand.

60. WHAT IS HYPERINFLATION?

DURING A HYPERINFLATIONARY period in Argentina, when the currency was losing its value at an alarming rate, it was joked that it was cheaper to take a taxi than a bus, because the bus ride was paid for at the beginning, when the currency was still worth something, while the taxi ride was paid for at the end—after the currency had already lost its value.

Hyperinflation—an explosion in the prices of goods and services—is a symptom of an economy out of control. Hyperinflation has occurred all over the world: in Germany between the two world wars, and more recently in Israel and parts of Eastern Europe. But it has been most widespread in the debtor countries of Latin America, where it resulted primarily from government policies that attempted to satisfy political demands without increasing taxes.

When a profligate government finances spending by increased borrowing or by simply printing new currency, prices will increase as the new money enters the economy. The expectation of runaway inflation fuels the fires of hyperinflation. Eventually, this wage and price spiral takes on a life of its own: prices rise, leading to a demand for increased wages, which results in higher prices. Imagine buying goods for a home or factory, or playing *The Price is Right*, when prices are increasing 150 percent a month. Even winning the lottery may not help when a million—or a billion—pesos doesn't even pay for next month's rent.

Hyperinflation's rising prices end up hurting poor people most, because their day-to-day expenses consume a significantly higher percentage of their total income. Some countries have tried to index all salaries and social service payments to the inflation rate, but this rarely keeps pace with the real increase in prices—"purchasing power" inevitably declines. Even though a salary is increased in nominal terms, what the salary will actually buy—called its *real* value—can decline.

Hyperinflation especially hurts those on fixed incomes, such as old age pensions. During hyperinflationary times, when prices are rising daily, a nest egg may become worthless in a few short months. With rent and food costs rising astronomically, stipends can become virtually worthless without cost-of-living increases.

Governments often refuse to take tough economic action against hyperinflation because they fear the political consequences of austerity plans or increased taxes. To keep large state work forces satisfied, many governments simply borrow more money. This allows them to keep from closing inefficient state industries or reducing bloated bureaucracies. Many overburdened governments keep the economy going by increasing the money supply even further, issuing more government debt, or printing even more money. As the government loses control of the economy, the self-perpetuating spiral of wage and price increases spins out of control.

61. WHAT ARE ECONOMIC AUSTERITY PLANS?

BELT TIGHTENING IS often the only way of solving a country's economic woes. When development banks and governments in wealthy countries are asked to help a struggling country, such as Mexico in the mid-1990s, they often insist on economic austerity plans. These plans usually call for a reduction in government spending, with rich and poor members of the population sharing the burdens equally.

The problem is that many developing countries are made up of a small rich elite and an enormous underclass, with the rich elite making the economic decisions and benefitting from previous loans. When Third World governments decide to tighten their belts, the burden is often shifted from the borrowing elites onto the poor, most of whom never benefitted from the previous loans and yet are asked to shoulder the burden of paying for them.

In many debtor countries, for example, the goods restricted under economic austerity plans are often those that are most important for a poor person's daily survival. Bread, fuel, other foodstuffs, and transportation are often the first items to have their prices raised in belt-tightening moves.

Third World governments often complain about the pressure from international organizations, such as the International Monetary Fund and the World Bank, which force them to adopt *structural adjustment* plans to manage their debt problems. Under most of these plans, the debtor country tries to reduce its domestic consumption of goods, such as shoes or orange juice, in order to export more. The increased exports are then supposed to be used to earn the foreign currency to pay the outstanding debt.

Most economic austerity plans reduce government subsidies for consumer products, such as food and transportation, making them more expensive. Governments also remove price controls, allowing the prices for products to rise along with inflation. At the same time, a cap is put on wages, which produces an effective wage cut. If the currency is devalued, it becomes even more expensive to import basic commodities such as flour and fuel.

These steps often lead to civil unrest. During the mid 1990s, for example, riots in the poor quarters of Cairo, civil disobedience in southern India, and outright rebellion by peasants in southern Mexico were direct consequences of economic austerity plans. Many economic restructuring plans, such as those imposed by the International Monetary Fund, improve life for the poor over the long run. But in most debt-ridden economies, it is especially difficult for them to bear the short-term burdens required by austerity plans.

Since many of the Third World poor are already living at subsistence levels, a small increase in the cost of essential goods could mean economic disaster. It is not very difficult to go without a new refrigerator—but it is very difficult to go without the food to put in it.

62. WHAT CAN BE DONE TO PROMOTE THIRD WORLD DEVELOPMENT?

MANY ENVIRONMENTALISTS SEE economic development in the Third World as a worst-case scenario. Industrial development, with new roads, automobiles, and pollution, is seen as adding to the world's economic and environmental problems.

However, there are hundreds of millions of people in the Third World suffering from malnutrition and substandard living conditions, for whom economic development is the only way out. In order to provide their people with the most basic services—clean water, sewage treatment, food, decent housing, and so forth—underdeveloped Third World countries will need to make their economies grow.

Economic expansion cannot possibly solve all of the Third World's problems, but without it, the future would be bleak indeed. Caught in a vicious cycle of low growth and falling export earnings, the people of many Third World countries face declining standards of living.

One of the first steps in encouraging development is to provide international markets for the goods produced in the world's poor regions. Exports of everything from rugs to fruit and from tourism to software allow Third World countries to earn the necessary currencies to import the goods and services that will fuel growth. International trade pacts, instead of exploiting the world's poor, can often help them with the first step in building a better life: earning a decent income.

Another step is to reduce the Third World's debt, which drains the resources of economies that can least afford it. One plan to reduce debt and supply additional funds to revive moribund Third World economies was formulated in the 1980s by U.S. Treasury secretary Nicholas Brady, who called for commercial banks to forgive part of the debt owed to them and to increase new lending. The basic goal of the Brady plan was to encourage economic growth in the Third World, through a net transfer of funds back to the developing countries.

Another way to promote Third World development is for the world's major development banks and funds, such as the World Bank and the International Monetary Fund, to provide "project loans" to rebuild the infrastructure in the Third World. The Inter-American Development Bank, for example, was set up to provide low-interest loans to developing countries in the Western Hemisphere. In this way, funds from wealthy countries are channeled to less-developed nations as "development loans."

Wealthy creditor governments also have the option of writing off their loans to poor countries, accepting the fact that it is never going to be repaid. France, for example, when confronted with the extreme poverty in several African debtor countries, decided to cancel the debt outright. The hope was that, by removing the debt burden entirely, further economic growth in the region could be encouraged.

Certain organizations have been set up to provide further assistance to Third World debtors. The Lomé Convention, for example, channels development aid from the European Union to poor Third World countries. The "Paris Club" also helps governments of debtor nations by "rescheduling" or delaying repayment of their loans until their economies are in better shape.

63. HOW IS GLOBAL ECONOMIC COOPERATION
ENCOURAGED?

JUST AS THE UNITED Nations Security Council can be used to solve the world's military and political disputes, many problems arising from global trade and investment can be solved through international groups and organizations.

One of the most active groups in formulating common economic goals is the Organization for Economic Co-Operation and Development (OECD). Besides providing statistics and documents on all aspects of the international economy, the OECD serves as a forum for discussions and coordination of economic policy. The OECD, headquartered in Paris, brings together the richest members of the world economy, including the United States, Canada, Japan, Australia, New Zealand, and most of the Western European economies.

International economic cooperation is also encouraged through periodic economic summits, including the "G-7" summit of the world's seven most powerful economies: the United States, Japan, Germany, Italy, Britain, France, and Canada. The G-7 summit began as a purely economic forum, but expanded quickly to cover a wide variety of international economic, political, and environmental issues, such as Eastern European economic reform and the protection of whales.

Because the world's economic problems are inseparable from political and military conflicts, it is essential to have political leaders meet periodically to try to solve economic problems. Iraq's decision to invade Kuwait, for example, leading to the gulf war in 1991, was principally motivated by an economic factor: access to Kuwait's oil fields and shipping facilities.

Basically, thorny international issues like global pollution, trade imbalances, and access to the sea's resources cannot be resolved by countries acting unilaterally, but depend on leaders working together, often through international groups and agencies.

64. WHAT IS THE WORLD TRADE ORGANIZATION?

ALTHOUGH A TRADE war may not be as destructive as a military war, in both cases people suffer, often including those people the war was meant to protect in the first place.

Every country wants access to the world's markets, but at times it may seem easier to close borders to trade rather than face strong foreign competition. When a country raises trade barriers, it can quickly turn into a full-scale trade war, as countries around the world retaliate with trade barriers of their own. Solving trade disputes is critical, because they can often escalate into global economic battles or even all-out military conflict.

The closest thing the world has to a universal trade law was negotiated under GATT, the General Agreement on Tariffs and Trade, ending in the signing of the "Uruguay Round" of negotiations in 1994. The GATT agreement, signed by more than

100 countries, expanded trade laws into many new areas. For the first time, protection was provided to exporters of a wide range of goods and services, including computer software, agriculture, textiles, and intellectual property rights.

Before investing time and money in developing new products, producers of intellectual property need to be assured that their investment will be protected from piracy in foreign markets. A Silicon Valley software producer, for example, or a Swiss pharmaceutical company, will be more likely to put the enormous investment into developing a new CD-ROM or a new AIDS vaccine if they know that they will be able to sell these goods in foreign markets such as China and Brazil. Without the worldwide protection of intellectual property provided by these GATT agreements, many new products would never see the light of day.

One important decision of the GATT agreements was to form an international body, the World Trade Organization (WTO), to act as a policeman with real powers to force countries to comply with the trade agreements. Whereas GATT was just an "agreement," the WTO is a formal legal entity. It has its headquarters in the old GATT building on the shores of Lake Geneva. The WTO's greatest strength is its real power to keep countries from unilaterally erecting trade barriers, such as quotas or tariffs, on imports.

Whereas previously GATT had to rely on voluntary compliance from its members, its new successor can force its members to follow its rules. If a country wants to benefit from trade with other WTO members—and essentially every country in the world economy has joined—it will not be allowed to erect any supplementary barriers to trade. In an extreme case, the WTO can use an independent appeals body to force compliance. Before 1993, GATT was a policeman without a gun, resolving trade

disputes by consensus. By providing its successor with the am-
munition to force compliance, GATT has transformed itself into
an effective force to regulate world trade.

If a country chooses not to respect the decisions of the
World Trade Organization—and every country has the right to
drop out of the WTO at any time— it risks cutting itself off from
the world economy, with an eventual loss of trade, jobs, and
economic growth.

65. WHAT ARE REGIONAL DEVELOPMENT BANKS?

WHEN A NEIGHBORHOOD bank decides to pro-
vide extra loans to build local homes and businesses, the
whole community usually benefits from the increased economic
activity. In the same way, the world's *regional development
banks* provide development funds for needy countries. These development loans serve to channel funds from the rich economies
to the "have-nots."

Development banks are not ordinary profit-oriented
banks. They do not take deposits, for example, but are funded
by large capital commitments and loans from developed nations, such as the United States, Japan, and Switzerland. These
funds are then lent at a low rate of interest to needy countries.

Development bank loans often include a grace period of
two to seven years before the borrower starts to pay back the
original amount borrowed, called the principal. This provides

time for the funded project, a hydroelectric dam, for example, to start making money before the principal payments begin.

The biggest regional development bank is the Inter-American Development Bank (IADB), based in Washington, D.C. Funded primarily by countries in the Western Hemisphere, the IADB provides loans for development projects in the poor countries of Latin America and the Caribbean.

The Asian Development Bank (ADB) was set up in 1966 to foster economic growth in Asia and the Pacific region. Headquartered in the Philippines, the ADB provides most of its loans for agricultural projects in countries such as Indonesia, Pakistan, and Thailand.

The African Development Bank (AfDB), the smallest of the development banks, is based in the Ivory Coast. Its loans are used mainly for public utilities, transportation, and agricultural projects in the poorest regions of Africa.

The European Investment Bank (EIB) provides funds for local projects in Western Europe, such as the Channel tunnel. Following the decision of the Eastern European countries to become free-market economies, the European Bank for Reconstruction and Development (EBRD) was set up in London to provide massive amounts of development aid to countries such as Poland, Hungary, Slovakia, and Lithuania.

66. WHAT ARE THE IMF AND THE WORLD BANK?

WHEN MEXICO'S ECONOMY faced impending collapse in the mid-1990s, it turned to the International Monetary Fund (IMF) for an injection of emergency funds. On the other side of the earth, the World Bank was providing funds to rebuild the Gaza Strip and to restore production in private-sector companies in Poland and other formerly communist countries in Eastern Europe.

These "sister" institutions, the World Bank and the IMF, located across the street from each other in Washington, D.C., serve many roles, including supervising the world economy and providing "last resort" assistance to economies in need.

The International Bank for Reconstruction and Development (IBRD), referred to simply as the World Bank, provides development aid to the world's underdeveloped countries. The IMF concentrates on providing advice and temporary funds for countries with economic difficulties.

The World Bank's first activity after being set up in 1945 was to channel funds from the United States and other nations into the reconstruction of postwar Europe. Its first loans, for example, were to rebuild war-torn Holland, Denmark, and France. The World Bank now provides most of its loans to countries in the Third World, and receives funding from the now-wealthy nations it was initially designed to assist.

Like the regional development banks, the World Bank receives its funds from rich member countries. This backing provides it with the credit to borrow cheaply on the world's capital markets. One billion dollars provided by the United States, for example, gives the World Bank the capital to borrow another 20 billion dollars to be used for loans. In this way, the World Bank can provide funds to the developing world at extremely favorable rates.

Although many World Bank projects have been criticized for destroying the environment—dams and highways in the Amazon, for example—most of its projects have been specifically targeted to help the poorest people of the developing world. To address the underlying causes of poverty in many developing nations, the World Bank often relies on the International Monetary Fund to encourage debtor countries to make difficult economic reforms.

Like a doctor called in at the last minute, the IMF is often asked to resuscitate ailing economies. This "structural adjustment" process is a crucial first step before receiving development assistance from other sources. Acceptance of an IMF plan is usually seen as a sign that a nation is prepared to seriously address its economic ills, paving the way for long-term funding from the World Bank and other sources.

The economic medicine prescribed by the IMF is frequently painful, requiring debtor governments to reduce subsidies to inefficient state industries and often calling for strict anti-inflationary measures. These measures may provoke considerable unrest, as they often raise the prices of previously subsidized services such as food and transportation. During this difficult restructuring process, the IMF often provides temporary "standby" loans to keep the country afloat until more long-term funding can be arranged.

67. HOW IS CORRUPTION PART OF THE WORLD ECONOMY?

FOR BUSINESSES AND governments in many countries around the world, corruption is a way of life—and corruption can take many forms. Government officials, for example, may not approve imports or exports without some sort of payment. Or, before signing any contract with an international partner, some company presidents may insist that a certain amount of money be deposited in a secret Swiss bank account. Similarly, military procurement officers may refuse to pay for shipments of arms without a large "gratuity."

Those who accept these payoffs point out that their salaries are extremely low precisely because it is assumed that their income will be supplemented by bribes, just as a waiter in a restaurant will accept a lower salary knowing that a large portion of the day's income will come from tips. "Gratuity" in the United States, *mordida* in Mexico, *baksheesh* in Egypt, *dash* in Kenya: many business deals would be impossible without some sort of supplemental payment.

For many businesspeople, it often seems impossible to compete abroad without getting dirty. Imagine trying to get good service in a restaurant if the waiters all know you are not going to give them a tip at the end of the meal. The main problem in doing business in many Third World countries is that the volume of undercover payments has reached crisis proportions. In China and Nigeria, for example, free-market reforms have been seriously jeopardized by corrupt business practices.

How can honest businesspeople avoid corruption? One way is to have a clear law from the mother country specifically forbidding bribery in business dealings abroad. The United States, for example, clearly prohibits international bribery through the Foreign Corrupt Practices Act. The goal is simple: if foreigners know that businesspeople are prohibited by their home country from providing bribes, they often will not ask for one. International efforts, such as Berlin-based Transparency International (TI), also try to fight graft by calling for greater visibility for all international business dealings.

Antibribery laws do not necessarily reduce a country's competitiveness. Often, firms doing business abroad can avoid bribery by working more closely with local partners who have already established business and family ties within the local community. These local partnerships may actually provide additional business expertise and succeed in opening doors that may not have opened otherwise.

68. WHAT IS MONEY LAUNDERING?

THE WORLD'S CRIMINALS need to periodically recycle their "dirty money" so that it can be used in the economy at large without anyone knowing about its illegal past. A drug dealer, for example, may end a day's work with a large amount of cash that needs to be deposited or otherwise spent.

Since there is a limit to the number of luxury automobiles or Miami condominiums a drug dealer can buy without creating suspicion, illicit earnings need to be put into a bank—to be available for future use. A money laundering scheme, therefore, essentially turns large sums of illegally earned funds into "respectable" money. The key to any money laundering scheme is to get the money into legitimate bank accounts without alerting law-enforcement officials to the money's illicit past. Once the money is in a legitimate account, it can then be transferred around the world without interference from the authorities.

This is possible because international bank transfers are just electronic messages. No money moves physically from Miami to Zurich to London and so forth. An international bank transfer simply instructs one bank to credit money to one account, while debiting another. The sheer size of these international computerized transfers, often exceeding $1 trillion per day, makes them difficult to control. The illegal transfers disappear in a sea of legal ones.

One popular money-laundering practice is to make hundreds of small deposits into a bank account, rather than a single large deposit, which would be reported to law-enforcement agencies. Another alternative is to mix illegal deposits with legal ones, channeling illegally earned money through legitimate businesses. A restaurant that does not accept credit cards, for example, deposits a large amount of cash each day into bank accounts. These transfers can often serve as a cover for deposits of illicit funds.

The currency of choice for most drug-related and other illegal transactions, such as prostitution and arms smuggling, is the U.S. dollar. This partly explains why more than half the U.S. greenbacks printed cannot be found anywhere in the U.S. economy. Drug lords in the Far East, prostitutes in Eastern Europe, and black market currency dealers in Latin America all make heavy use of the U.S. dollar for their illegal activities.

Laundering U.S. dollars is easier than laundering other international currencies. U.S. currency, mainly twenty-and hundred-dollar bills, is prized for its liquidity: dollars can be exchanged almost anywhere in the world without raising suspicion. Because of the size and stability of the U.S. economy, the U.S. dollar has become the "currency of choice" for most players in the underground economies of the world.

69. HOW DOES A SWISS BANK ACCOUNT WORK?

SWITZERLAND IS ONE of the few countries in the world that guarantees, by law, the secrecy of its bank accounts. As long as the client of a Swiss bank has not done anything considered illegal in Switzerland, the bank cannot reveal the client's identity to anyone. Switzerland is also seen as a safe financial haven in a turbulent world.

During World War II, for example, many families from war-torn France, Italy, and Germany were able to keep their savings secure in Swiss banks. Many Europeans still consider having a bank account in Zurich, Basel, Lugano, or Geneva to be a sign of financial security.

Opening a legal, numbered Swiss bank account is still relatively easy to do, usually involving nothing more than going to Switzerland, filling out a few forms, and making a deposit. Swiss bankers are known to be dependable, trustworthy, and, above all, discreet. These qualities made Switzerland a world banking center, but they have also made Switzerland a center for money laundering.

Swiss bank accounts are useful for money laundering

schemes because once money passes through a respectable Swiss bank it is accepted anywhere in the world. Many criminals in the world economy, from Russian black-marketeers to Third World dictators, prefer putting their money in Switzerland because of its reputation for honesty and stability.

However, most people holding Swiss bank accounts do not use them to launder illegally earned money. They merely want their legally earned funds to be safe and free from government control and taxes at home. Since they can count on the Swiss to be discrete, citizens from turbulent or high-tax economies often open Swiss bank accounts.

Swiss bankers will not reveal the accounts of clients accused simply of avoiding taxes. Since tax evasion is not considered "illegal" in Switzerland—it is only a civil, not a criminal, offense—earnings in a Swiss bank account remain secret from authorities in the client's home country. Essentially, foreigners with legally earned money—as long as they break no Swiss laws—can keep their funds in Swiss bank accounts without fear.

The guarantee of Swiss banking secrecy is often used by unscrupulous clients for a wide variety of shady international activities. In the case of the Iran-contra scandals, for example, the person responsible for handling the secret arms sales to Iran placed the money in Swiss banks before sending it on to the contras in Central America. These bank accounts were subsequently opened at the request of the U.S. government.

The Swiss authorities have recently decided to require every Swiss bank to know the beneficial owner of money in their accounts. Only those funds earned legally would then be allowed to benefit from the Swiss banking secrecy laws.

70. WHAT IS A TAX HAVEN?

THE TERM *TAX HAVEN* usually conjures up images of palm trees and shady criminals sitting around swimming pools drinking banana daiquiris.

In fact, the purpose of a tax haven is not to facilitate illegal international activities but to provide a low-tax environment to attract business to otherwise overlooked economic centers. The most popular tax havens are found on islands in the Caribbean, such as the Netherlands Antilles or the British Virgin Islands. Tax havens are also found in the Pacific, in small countries in Europe, and in Central America.

Many small countries, such as the Cayman Islands or the Isle of Man, require little or no taxes from the foreigners who come there to set up operations. It is a lucrative opportunity that many businesses and individuals can't pass up. Just as many U.S. companies choose to register their headquarters in Delaware to take advantage of lower taxes and favorable legal requirements, many international companies set up subsidiaries in tax havens to achieve the same benefits.

Many companies from Europe and North America also use subsidiaries in tax havens such as the Netherlands Antilles to issue bonds. These "offshore" operations allow many companies to raise funds in the international capital markets, such as the Eurobond market, with a minimum of regulations and taxes. This significantly lowers their cost of borrowing.

Individuals also like the anonymity of having a company in

a tax haven. This allows them to choose whether to report their income, booked through the offshore company, to the tax authorities in their home country. Even if this tax avoidance is illegal in the home country, it is usually not considered to be illegal in the tax haven itself.

Because of their anonymity, most tax havens attract some illegal activity. Drug lords, black marketeers, and other "shady" figures often use companies in tax havens to hide their activities and bank accounts. Most activity in the world's tax havens, however, fully complies with international laws and regulations.

71. HOW DO INTERNATIONAL CRIMINALS ESCAPE PROSECUTION?

THE MASTERMIND OF Britain's famous Briggs train robbery was able to escape from the scene of the crime and flee to Rio, knowing that he could live there in freedom.

How was this possible? The British authorities were helpless to act because there was no treaty between Britain and Brazil requiring the transfer of such criminals. Although Brazil does extradite most criminals to face trial in their home countries, it is one of many countries in the world economy that does not extradite all criminals for all types of crime.

International criminals rarely get away with murder, which is clearly illegal in every country. International drug traffickers are also widely extraditable, and many countries, such as Colombia and Mexico, have sent traffickers to face prosecution in the United States. But different laws in different countries often hinder authorities from tracking down and prosecuting criminals who make their living in the interlinked global economy.

What is perfectly legal in one country—buying and selling foreign currencies, for example—may be strictly prohibited in another. When a country attempts to extradite accused criminals from foreign hideaways, their pleas may fall on deaf ears. Authorities abroad are usually reluctant to extradite people accused of activities they do not consider to be a criminal offense.

Tax evasion, severely punished in the United States, is not considered an extraditable offense in many countries. For example, an American living in Switzerland who is accused of U.S. tax evasion—a civil rather than a criminal offense in Switzerland—would not normally be extradited.

Prosecuting international criminals is most difficult when the laws they are accused of breaking do not even exist abroad. In many countries, pirate copies of Janet Jackson tapes and Microsoft software have often been sold without any penalty whatsoever. Only when the GATT accords prohibited pirating and copyright infringement did illegal copying of cassettes and software become a crime in many parts of the world. As long as countries have different customs and laws, some international criminals will always be able to escape prosecution.

72. WHAT ARE BLACK MARKETS?

ILLEGAL OR SEMI-LEGAL goods and services, ranging from elephant tusks to prostitution and drugs, are traded daily on the world's black markets.

In countries with currency restrictions, for example, black market currency exchanges have flourished. When a government tries to limit an activity, even one as innocuous as currency trading, it will go underground and become part of the world's black market. In Brazil, when trading of foreign currencies was considered illegal, rates were still published in the newspapers as the "parallel" market. In other parts of the world, trading in endangered animals, rare tropical woods, and other restricted goods is often carried out with the collusion of corrupt local officials.

The world economy is also full of semi-legal or "gray market" activities, such as transfers and deposits of legally earned but undeclared funds that have to be hidden from the authorities at home. For example, normally law-abiding Italian, French, and Latin American citizens have transferred money to bank accounts abroad during periods of domestic instability and exchange restrictions.

The formation of a shadow economy, where "gray money" transfers need to be kept hidden even though they are legal, has opened the door to a wide variety of abuses. In the United States and Europe, for example, illegally earned drug money finds its way into the gray economy, where it is hidden among the large quantities of legal money. The volume of gray money transfers, estimated to be over $1 trillion per year, more than the GDP of most countries, is so big that regulators cannot monitor it all. The "black" money gets lost in the sea of gray money transfers.

The best solution for many gray market and black market abuses is concerted consumer efforts on a global basis. If people refuse to import illegally made products, such as products made with slave labor or endangered-animal parts, the market for these illegally made products will cease to exist. Some consumer groups are, therefore, promoting the use of certificates on goods attesting to their legal origin. By working with countries that have been less than vigilant in the past, the wealthy members of the world economy can use their economic leverage to end much of the world's black market activity.

73. HOW IS SLAVERY PART OF THE WORLD ECONOMY?

WHEN A BANGKOK toy factory was destroyed by fire in 1993, international attention was focused on the fact that most of those killed were child laborers.

Every year, thousands of children in rural areas of Third World countries become virtual slaves when they are "sold" by their parents to employment agents, who pay a fee to the impoverished parents. These children are then taken by their new "owners" to work in factories producing low cost goods.

The double tragedy of the toy-factory fire in Bangkok is that the survivors, often children ten to fourteen years old, ended up even worse off. First, they lost their jobs after an international boycott closed down their employers' factories. Instead of being returned to their families, however, many children were put to work as child prostitutes in the hundreds of brothels throughout Thailand.

It is one of the dirty little secrets of the world economy that many employees do not have the freedom to leave their jobs. Slavery, although officially illegal, is tolerated to some degree in almost every country in the world, including many of the advanced industrial economies.

In the United States, for example, many agricultural workers are hired for a "season." During their employment, they are allowed—even encouraged—to make purchases from the company store. Often, these purchases consist of nonessential goods such as cigarettes and liquor at highly inflated prices. By the end of the season, a worker may owe more than the amount earned from salary, "owing their souls to the company store." These employees are then told they will not be allowed to leave their jobs until these outstanding bills are paid off, with the threat of physical force preventing any employee from fleeing.

In rural Asia, it is estimated that during the 1980s more than a million women and children had been sold into slavery. In Thailand, for example, children often end up as "sex slaves" when their impoverished parents in the countryside are paid a fee by "employment agents" who tell the parents their children will be brought to the city to work as waitresses or will be given a job in a factory. Many of these children end up working as prostitutes in the sex industry.

In India, many young boys have been sold by their parents to work in the rug industry. As in Thailand, their parents are paid a fee for releasing them to "employment agents." It often takes many years for the boys to pay off the fee originally paid to their parents. During these years of virtual slavery, they work long hours and live in miserable conditions.

International outcry, however, can be effective. By organizing consumer boycotts of products made by slave labor, consumers in the world's wealthy countries have been effective in reducing the use of slave labor. In China, many prisoners are forced to work in factories producing consumer goods for Western markets. By refusing to buy these products, consumers have reduced the use of these virtual slaves—at least in the production of the products sold in the West. In India, the use of child slave labor in the rug industry has also been reduced by Western boycotts. Many rugs coming from India now have tags that certify that they are not made by slave labor.

Like many problems in the global economy, the use of child labor is not easily remedied. In almost every agricultural society, children are often used to help the family with the planting and harvesting of crops on their own land, with no apparent harm to their health or educational growth.

Likewise, unskilled workers in developing countries can often survive on extremely low wages. Many consumers in wealthy industrial nations find it scandalous that workers are paid only a dollar a day to produce athletic shoes that are then sold for a hundred times that amount in shops in London, Seattle, or Osaka. When judged by Western standards their salaries seem "obscene," but when judged by local standards—food and lodging may cost much less than a dollar per day—they begin to look reasonable. For an unskilled worker in a country with an extremely low cost of living, a "poorly paid" job may, in fact, be a way to a better life.

Every employee in the world economy, however, should

have the freedom to choose. If a child or worker in another country is forced to work under conditions indistinguishable from slavery, it is up to consumers and governments around the world to stop the offending practices, using economic force, if necessary. Consumers can exercise their right to choose which products to buy, sometimes even organizing boycotts. By refusing to support carefully selected products, goods, and services, consumers can play a large part in ending the practice of slavery in the global economy.

74. HOW IS THE ENVIRONMENT AFFECTED BY THE WORLD ECONOMY?

ALTHOUGH IT IS not always obvious, every one of the world's manmade environmental problems is the direct result of an economic decision. Industrial pollution, for example, exists because it is more expensive to clean up pollutants than it is to dump them into the water and the air.

No one wants to pollute, but environmental protection, like all other economic decisions, involves an economic tradeoff. Companies, countries, and even consumers must decide how much they are ready to pay to keep the environment clean and healthy. This decision is, essentially, an economic one.

Industrial nations have often treated the world and its resources as if they were disposable commodities. This ignores a basic concept of economics: all factors of production—whether land, labor, or clean water—are scarce commodities and have a price that should be factored into every business and economic decision. Clean air and water, for example, was once thought of as limitless. In fact, they have been rapidly "depleted" by burgeoning populations and rampant industrial development. They need to be treated like any other scarce resource.

Governments and consumer groups play an important role in protecting the environment, puting in place economic incentives that force companies and governments to change environmentally unsound practices and policies. When a company is forced to pay for its pollution, for example, it will think twice before discharging its waste into the air and water. And when a government is forced to include the depletion of natural resources in its calculation of total economic activity—creating an "environmental GDP," for example—it may think twice about wasting precious forests and mineral deposits.

Like all sectors of the world economy, environmental protection is not limited by national barriers. What one country does to alter the environment has an effect on others. Industrial waste rising above Chicago comes down as acid rain in Quebec; chemicals entering the water in Basel, Switzerland, end up as pollution in the North Sea. Whether it is deforestation, depletion of the ozone layer, or dumping of radioactive waste in the ocean, every major case of environmental pollution is international in nature.

Environmental protection can by no means be confined to modern industrial economies. In fact, the people of the Third World are those most affected by environmental issues such as global warming and deforestation. The low-lying regions of Bangladesh, for example, would be the first to be hit by any rise in the level of the world's oceans as a result of global warming. Furthermore, the costs of protecting the environment are especially high for the developing countries where many natural resources have been depleted and vast areas have been polluted in the drive for economic growth.

A healthy environment need not be incompatible with a prosperous economy. Indeed, some of the world's most destructive pollution has occurred in economically backward countries, such as in the former Soviet bloc of Eastern Europe. In contrast, some of the world's cleanest air and water can be found in the most advanced industrial economies, such as Canada and Sweden. By looking at environmental issues from a global perspective, it becomes clear that protecting the environment allows the world to sustain healthy economic growth in the years to come.

75. WHAT ARE POLLUTION RIGHTS?

ONE OF THE most difficult problems facing the world economy is how to increase the standard of living for growing populations without destroying the environment. A new concept has emerged to reduce the amount of pollution in an economy without destroying economic growth. The United States and several other countries have begun limiting pollution in a given area and then allowing local industries and other companies to buy and sell the *pollution rights* among themselves.

Many environmental groups have come to support such systems because they come as close as possible to solving two seemingly irreconcilable goals: economic growth and a clean environment. The key to the pollution rights plan is to induce companies and other polluters to decrease their output of emissions in the most efficient way possible.

Faced with the prospect of reducing economic activity in order to reduce pollution, many countries have balked. They simply cannot afford to shut down plants producing shelter, clothing, and other essential goods for their growing populations. Although in the past it seemed fair to force everyone to reduce pollution equally, putting limits on each polluter's output, the result was economically catastrophic. In fact, under previous antipollution campaigns, governments ended up hurting the economy by giving the "right to pollute" to all producers, whether or not they were efficient and useful to the economy at large.

Instead of requiring all polluters to reduce their output equally, the new pollution rights plans recognize that there are differences between polluters: some should be allowed to grow and provide jobs and products for an expanding economy and some should simply go out of business.

In a free-market system, there is an efficient way of telling the "good" from the "bad" polluters: the invisible hand of the marketplace. Those companies that should not be polluting at all are the inefficient ones that provide the least production per amount of pollution. There is really no such thing as a "good" polluter, but those that produce needed goods for the economy should be allowed to stay in business while the unproductive polluters should be induced to go out of business or at least reduce their activities.

An efficiently run wheelchair factory, for example, will produce less pollution per product than an inefficient one. Under a traditional antipollution plan, a government would have limited the production at both plants, allowing both the inefficient factory and the efficient one to continue producing and polluting at lower levels. Under previous plans, governments gave a "pollution" right to everyone, regardless of their efficiency in producing needed goods for the economy.

Under a "pollution rights" plan, an efficient producer can "buy" the right to pollute from an inefficient one. In this way, the inefficient producer would be induced to reduce its production and pollution, and the efficient one uses the pollution "rights" to increase va@ALPHA:luable economic production.

76. WHAT IS A DEBT-FOR-NATURE SWAP?

TROPICAL FORESTS OR wildlife refuges around the world can be preserved by debt-for-nature swaps, which allow banks, environmental groups, and debtor countries to use economic tools to protect parts of the environment for future generations.

Since many poor countries do not even have the financial resources to repay their foreign loans, it is difficult to get them to spend money on "luxuries" such as nature parks or wildlife preserves. Environmental protection groups, however, have devised an ingenious method for getting poor debtor countries to protect their natural heritage.

Under a "debt-for-nature swap," a wealthy environmental group pays off a poor country's debt in exchange for a commitment to protect ecologically valuable land such as forests, wetlands, or regions rich in wildlife. They do this by buying bonds owed by debtor countries such as Columbia or Peru, and using their financial leverage to get considerable "bang" for their environmental buck.

In the world financial markets, many Third World loans are sold at a discount to their face value because no one expects poor debtor countries to repay all of their debt. Debt, like any other financial instrument, can be bought and sold on the open market. A bank, for example, can sell a Third World loan to another bank in the same way someone sells a bond or other forms of IOUs. The purchaser of the loan expects to get paid back, in part at least, by the original borrower.

Some doubtful loans to Third World countries can sell for as little as 10 percent of their original face value. An environmental group can, therefore, buy a $100 million loan for as little as $10 million. It may be worth $100 million to the debtor country but it is only worth $10 million to the bank selling it.

By going back to the debtor country, the environmental group can say, "Look, I own your loan worth $100 million. Instead of paying off the loan to me, use the money to set aside a large area of land as an ecological preserve." The debtor country is happy to agree, because the money destined to pay off the foreign loan can now be used within the country to protect the environment.

In the end, everyone is better off. The debtor country gains a nature park and a reduction in its foreign debt. International banks are happy to see their debt exposure reduced, even if it means getting only a part of their money back, and the environmental group has been able, for a reduced amount of money, to preserve an ecologically important part of the world for future generations.

77. HOW CAN ECONOMIC SANCTIONS AND INCENTIVES BE USED TO PROTECT THE ENVIRONMENT?

FROM THE ENDANGERED mountain gorillas of Africa to the vanishing trees and plants of the Amazon rain forest, natural resources around the world can be preserved using economic sanctions and incentives. Once it has been shown that precious wildlife and trees are worth more alive than dead, people will finally begin to change their environmentally—and economically—destructive behavior.

Until recently, the destruction of forests, rivers, and wildlife around the world has often been carried out in the name of economic progress. Many companies and governments were simply not aware of the fact that much long-term growth is dependent on a healthy environment.

The Amazon rain forest, for example, was being destroyed at an alarming rate during the 1980s largely because of misguided economic policy. Poorly conceived tax laws in Brazil provided an incentive for farmers to move into the Amazon and burn large areas of the rain forest to be used for crops or cattle grazing. These policies had questionable economic value and disastrous environmental consequences, including large quantities of carbon dioxide being dumped into the atmosphere. After considerable international outcry, the Brazilian government changed its environmentally and economically harmful policies.

Although a country's environmentally destructive actions can be changed in the short term by applying international political pressure, long-term changes can be brought about only by making a country aware of the economic value of preserving its natural resources.

By providing economic incentives, such as tourist income or exports of renewable products, countries can be made aware of the value of preserving precious natural resources. Instead of slaughtering elephant herds or mountain gorillas, for example, a country can create wildlife refuges to stimulate tourism. By periodically harvesting the fruits, nuts, and plants found in the rain forests, countries can also earn valuable foreign exchange. The income from medicinal and food exports from a living rain forest can often surpass the questionable profit of burning the trees. In the end, the whole world breathes a lot easier.

Another effective way of forcing a government or a company to change environmentally harmful practices is to threaten economic sanctions, such as boycotts and trade restrictions. The threat of a consumer boycott on the world markets, for example, can be effective because it provides the most powerful economic incentive around: the loss of profits. Drift-net tuna fishing, for example, was halted or altered to protect the porpoises only after consumers threatened to boycott the tuna of the offending companies.

Governments can also impose trade restrictions, such as embargoes that prohibit the import of goods from countries with environmentally harmful practices. Trade restrictions, however, often end up provoking the targeted country into erecting trade barriers of its own, ultimately hurting everyone. But when many nations band together to send a clear environment-friendly message, threats of retaliation often lose their punch.

Environmental agreements reached at the United Nations are also effective because they are voted on by all of the member countries. Although these resolutions are usually nonbinding, direct enforcement is unnecessary if broad worldwide support for them can be obtained. Often, the best solution is found in international summits, where all nations concerned can sit down and reach some form of negotiated settlement. In many ways, the global environment's future depends on rational economic growth managed through international cooperation.

What exactly are derivatives? What is an ADR? What is hot money? When these terms come up in the course of our daily lives, we may have to refresh our memories. Business discussions, politics, and the daily news are increasingly dominated by the world economy. If we are going to be effective players in this new world, we need to speak the language of the global economy. This list is intended to be as light and informative as possible and can be used like a card file to which we can return, time and time again.

American Depository Receipt (ADR). To make things easier for North American investors who want to buy shares of a foreign company, banks buy the foreign shares and hold them on deposit. The bank then issues a receipt, called an ADR, that gives the holder the right to the foreign shares and dividends. The advantage for the investor: everything is denominated in U.S. dollars. Most ADRs are traded on the over-the-counter market.

Arbitrage. Giving new meaning to the expression "It pays to shop around!": when there are price differences for the same product in different markets, an arbitrager will buy large quantities in the cheap market and sell them in the expensive one. The practice of arbitrage is quite simple and has been used for centuries to make profits and to keep the markets efficient. Recently, takeover specialists have used the techniques of arbitrage to buy shares of undervalued companies in order to resell them at a higher price once the companies have been restructured.

Asset. On a balance sheet, assets are positives, liabilities are negatives. The assets of most companies include financial assets such as cash and securities, fixed assets such as buildings and machinery, and nontangible assets such as goodwill, brand names, and copyrights.

Asset stripping. Sometimes two plus two is more than four: when an undervalued company is acquired, its assets can be sold in pieces to make more money than it costs to acquire the whole company. Asset stripping is a key factor in the takeover game, where the proceeds from asset sales are used to pay off the debt incurred when acquiring the company.

Balance of payments. A measure of a country's total international trade, the balance of payments counts all trade in goods, services, and money. It is called a "balance" because the transfer of goods and services is always balanced by transfers of money in the opposite direction. The trade in goods and services, measured by the current account, is balanced by transfers of money, measured by the capital account.

Balance sheet. Listing all of the company's assets and liabilities, a balance sheet provides a snapshot of a company at any given time. When the company has more assets than liabilities, the stockholders are happy. Their share of the balance sheet, the difference between assets and liabilities, is called shareholders' equity.

Bankruptcy. A bankrupt company is one that can't pay its debts. In some countries, bankrupt companies are given an opportunity to restructure in order to pay off their creditors. This is called Chapter Eleven in the United States and administration in Britain. If the company can find no other solution, it is liquidated. Its assets are then sold to pay as many of the creditors as possible.

Barter. Exchanging one good for another, barter allows traders to avoid the problems of unconvertible currencies. In most developed countries, barter is unnecessary because it is much easier to use money to buy and sell goods and services. But in many countries with artificially fixed exchange rates, the local currency cannot be converted on the international markets. Barter is often the only alternative for someone wanting to do business in countries with no hard currencies such as U.S. dollars or German marks.

Basis point. A hundred of these make one percentage point. Bond markets have become so finely tuned that it is no longer enough to talk about yields, or prices, going up a quarter or a sixteenth of a percent. They can move by as little as a hundredth of a percent, or one basis point. A quarter percent rise in a bond's yield, for example, is twenty-five basis points.

Bear market/bull market. A bear, growling and pessimistic, is used to describe a declining market. A bull, charging optimistically ahead, symbolizes a rising market.

Bearer bond. Bearer bonds are the ultimate transferable security. There is no owner's name or registration for a bearer bond, so the holder has the right to receive the full value of the bond and any interest payments. International spies and villains in James Bond movies like to get paid with bearer bonds because they can be cashed with no questions asked. Most international securities, such as Eurobonds, are issued in bearer form.

Big Bang. After London's stock market was deregulated in the mid-1980s, the world's financial community looked for an explosion of banking and financial services. Many international banks and trading operations moved to London to take advantage of the opportunities for trading large amounts of securities with no restrictions or taxes imposed by the local authorities.

Bilateral trade agreements. Bilateral trade agreements, between two countries who come to an understanding on how trade in goods and services are to be controlled, serve as a first step to more sweeping, multilateral accords.

Black market, black economy. Black markets spring up wherever a desired good or service is prohibited or severely controlled. In some countries, black markets—such as currency exchange offices—are tolerated with little or no police interference. In countries with artificially controlled currencies, for example, the black market rates usually reflect the true market price. The black economy consists of all those underground transactions that, because of their illegality, go unreported.

Bond. The ultimate IOU, a bond is a piece of paper that says, "I, the borrower, agree to pay you, the owner, a certain amount of money at a certain time in the future." The pieces of paper we call bonds—and their electronic counterparts—can be bought and sold among investors. Whoever owns the bond holds the right to receive the payments agreed to when the bond was issued. These payments often include an interest payment. Zero-coupon bonds pay no interest rate but are sold at a discount to provide a higher return to investors when the bonds are paid back.

Bourse. The word *bourse*, which means "purse" in French, has come to mean "stock market" around the world.

Bridge loan. Bridge loans, as the name implies, are loans that cover a short span of time, allowing the borrower to receive funds until more long-term loans can be arranged. The International Monetary Fund and the Bank for International Settlements usually provide bridge loans to poor countries trying to arrange loans with the World Bank and other long-term lenders.

Broker. Like a real estate agent who brings together buyers and sellers for a fee, a broker acts as a go-between in financial transactions. Most brokers, like stock brokers, receive a commission based on the volume of securities traded. A dealer, on the other hand, has an inventory of goods than can be sold to investors. Some investment bankers fill both roles and are called, not surprisingly, broker/dealers.

Bundesbank. Germany's central bank, the Bundesbank, is responsible for safeguarding the German currency and controlling the economy. Bundesbank means "Federal Bank" in German. The Bundesbank is located in Frankfurt, Germany's financial capital.

Call option. A call option gives the right to buy something at a certain price. Like other options, a call option can only be used, or exercised, for a certain length of time. An investor who thinks the price of a stock will go up will buy a call option. As the price of the underlying security goes up, so does the price of the call option. International investors can buy options on such diverse instruments as stocks, commodities, futures, and foreign currencies.

Capital gains tax. An increase in the price of assets such as stocks or real estate is a capital gain. An investment in stocks will provide a capital gain if the price of the shares goes up. Capital gains are usually taxed at a different rate from other income, such as interest, dividend payments, and earned income.

Capital markets. A capital market is an exchange or a group of exchanges where such securities as bonds and other long-term debt instruments are traded. Much capital market trading is not done in official exchanges, but on trading floors in banks around the world, connected electronically to form one big international market.

Cash crops/food crops. "Give a starving man a fish and he will eat for a day; give him a fishing pole and he will hunger no more." In developing countries, a farmer's crops used to feed the farmer's family are called food crops. Cash crops are crops that are not consumed, but are sold to provide money to buy clothing, shelter, and other items.

Cash flow. A quick measure of the money coming into or going out of a company during a given period is called cash flow. It gives a clear idea of a company's true earnings because it excludes accounting tools, such as depreciation, that allow a company to reduce the profits reported on its books, in order to pay less tax. Cash flow factors out all of the accounting tricks and looks at what a company really earned.

Centrally planned economies. In a centrally planned economy, the bureaucrats make all the decisions. The state has the authority to decide who produces what and how much. Prices and resource allocation are also decided by the central decision-making bodies. The goal is to make economic decisions more rational and equitable, but the result is often increased waste and inefficiency. Centrally planned economies are also called command economies or, simply, planned economies.

Chapter Seven, Chapter Eleven. These are the two most important concepts in the book of bankruptcy. Chapter Eleven, called administration in Britain, allows a bankrupt company to try to work out its troubles. It is hoped that with time and new finances, the company will be back on its feet again. In Chapter Seven, called receivership in Britain, the company is liquidated, and the assets are sold off to pay off as many of the company's debts as possible.

The City, Wall Street, Bahnhofstrasse. The part of London where the major banks and securities houses are located is called the City of London. The British financial community is therefore commonly referred to as "the City." In New York, the markets use the term "Wall Street" to describe the financial community as a whole, while in Zurich it's the "Bahnhofstrasse" and in Tokyo the "Kabuto-cho." When Venice was the center of the world economy, the banks were all found on the Rialto. Hence, Shylock's famous line in Shakespeare's *The Merchant of Venice*: "What news on the Rialto?"

Classical economics. The basic idea of classical economics is that an economy will always move toward an equilibrium. Like a well-balanced seesaw, the idea of classical economists such as Adam Smith, David Ricardo, and John Stuart Mill was that when too many people are looking for jobs, wages would go down until everyone became employed. The problem, as John Maynard Keynes pointed out in the twentieth century, is that wages rarely go down. If that is the case, classical economists may just have to "assume" full employment.

Commercial banks. A commercial bank takes deposits and makes loans. In the United States and Japan, commercial banks have been prohibited by law from getting involved in investment banking activities, such as underwriting share offerings and trading stocks and bonds. The distinction is being blurred as commercial banks are now being increasingly allowed to move into previously prohibited investment banking territory. By the beginning of the 1990s, nine of the ten largest commercial banks in the world were Japanese.

Commodity. The term *commodity* is used to refer to raw materials or primary products, such as gold or orange juice concentrate. A commodity is easily traded on the world markets because it is relatively homogeneous: gold from Siberia is basically the same as gold from Nevada. Commodities can be traded in spot transactions for immediate delivery, or they can be traded for future delivery, or through options. Other examples of commodities traded on the world markets: wool, silver, tin, platinum, beef, oil, wheat, and the proverbial pork bellies.

The Common Market. The common name for the European Union, the Common Market refers to the world's largest single trading bloc uniting European economies from Sweden to Portugal and from Ireland to Greece.

Communism. The idea of "from each according to his abilities, to each according to his needs," was to create a society with total equality. This utopian idea was developed during the nineteenth century by economic philosophers, such as Karl Marx, who tried to find an alternative to the terrible abuses of the capitalist system during the early years of the Industrial Revolution. The answer, according to Marx, was a revolution of the proletariat: the workers of the world were supposed to unite and create a utopia, where everyone was equal.

Comparative advantage. The trade theory of comparative advantage is based on the practical idea that if a country excels in one activity, the others should not try to duplicate it—they should each do what they do best. By trading goods and services, everyone should be better off: the country that makes the best wine should make it for everyone and the others can spend their time making bread, cheese, bottles, and so forth. In the end, everyone can sit down to a better economic "meal" with products from around the world.

Consumer price index (CPI). Governments keep track of the prices in a "basket" of goods, in order to determine the inflation in an economy. This index, called the CPI in the United States, is supposed to indicate how much an average person's expenses go up each month. This measure is then used to readjust fixed incomes such as pensions and social security payments. This "cost of living index" is called the "retail price index" in Britain.

Convertible bond. To make bonds or other securities more attractive to investors, companies sometimes allow them to be convertible, or exchangeable into something else of value, usually shares of the company. During the "life" of the bond, the owner of a convertible bond has the right, but not the obligation, to trade the bond for a fixed number of shares.

Corporate finance. When companies or governments need to borrow money, they usually turn to investment banks to find the best financing at the best price. The expense of this advice is often compensated by reduced borrowing costs on the international markets. The goal of a corporate finance team of advisers is to find the right mix of bonds, equity, swaps, and loans that allows the borrower to secure funding at the lowest possible cost.

Correction. For those who expect the market to continue rising, an unexplained drop in prices is called a temporary market "correction."

Cum. In Latin, *cum* means "with." A bond with a warrant still attached to it is therefore referred to as "cum." Similarly, a stock sold with the dividend still to be paid is called "cum dividend."

Currency. A mark, a yen, a buck, or a pound, printed money is the currency of advanced industrial economies. Most currencies are nothing more than a promise by a country's central bank, written on pretty paper. In the United States, the Federal Reserve's promise used to include the option to exchange the dollar for gold. Since 1973, this is no longer the case. Now most major currencies are only worth what other people— mainly traders in the markets—are willing to pay for them. International foreign exchange traders are ruthless in devaluing a currency if it looks as if inflation will make it worth less in the years to come.

Current account. A country's current account measures its international trade in goods and services over a given period. Current accounts measure "visible" trade, such as imports of apples and televisions, and "invisible" trade, such as financial services and dividends earned from investments abroad. The current account also includes private transfers, such as money sent home by someone working abroad. In addition, it includes official transfers, such as a country's payments to international organizations and interest payment on a country's foreign debt.

Datsu-sara. The Japanese had to invent a word to describe Japanese managers who adopted the Western practice of leaving a company to go their own way. Usually, Japanese workers are expected to remain faithful to one employer, and vice versa. *Datsu-sara* literally means "corporate dropout."

Debenture. A debenture is any bond backed only by the good credit of the corporation issuing it. It is an IOU that can be negotiated, bought, or sold by a wide variety of investors. The purchaser of a debenture relies on the "full faith and credit" of the issuer to be paid back. Some debentures are paid off only after other, more senior, creditors have been paid. These "subordinated" debentures usually provide a higher interest rate to reward the holder for the higher risk.

Debt ratio, debt/equity ratio. A company's health can often be detected by comparing how much it owes to how much it owns. The basic idea for debt ratios is that if the ratio is high, the company may have borrowed too much and will have trouble paying the interest when it comes due. A debt/equity ratio compares the company's debt to the equity its stockholders have invested. A company can improve its debt ratio by paying back loans, or by increasing its equity, which means getting stockholders to invest more money.

Default. When a company, or a country, is not able to pay its creditors on time, it is said to be in default. The interest payments on notes and bonds are usually the first to be stopped by a debtor in default. If no solution is found, the company files bankruptcy. A country in default essentially gives up future access to the world economy for further loans.

Deficit. Almost too good to be true, a deficit allows a government to spend what it does not earn. In the world economy, there are two major kinds of deficits: budget deficits and trade deficits. A government's budget deficit occurs when tax revenues are not enough to pay for spending. To cover a budget deficit, a government usually prints bonds and sells them to the public to make up the difference. A trade deficit is based on the same principle: a country runs a trade deficit when spending on imports exceeds income from exports.

Deflation. Deflation is an economic slowdown. If a country's inflation rate or trade deficit is too high, the government can cool down the economy by raising taxes and reducing spending. During deflation there is less pressure to spend, so prices stop rising and imports are reduced.

Demand. The part of economics relating to consumption is called demand. It tells us what consumers or businesses will buy at a given price. Many economists use supply and demand curves to explain the very simple idea that when prices change, consumers and producers change their behavior: when prices go up, more goods and services are supplied, but there is less demand from consumers. When prices go down, demand goes up but the supply is reduced. At a certain price level there will be an equilibrium of supply and demand.

Depreciation. The reduction of an asset's value over time is called depreciation. Tax authorities allow a company to reduce the value on their books of buildings and other capital goods, such as machinery, trucks, and copy machines. A company treats these depreciations as costs, which allows it to reduce reported earnings. Companies prefer to depreciate as much as they can as early as they can, in order to reduce taxes.

Depression. A prolonged economic slowdown is called a depression. It is marked by a steep decline in production and demand. As a result, companies go bankrupt and unemployment rises. The Great Depression of the 1930s, caused in part by a worldwide trade war, made it clear how interconnected the world economy had become. Governments can usually avoid depressions by providing the necessary stimulus, such as an increase in the money supply or an increase in government spending.

Deregulation. *"Que será, será*—whatever will be, will be." When a government wants to encourage competition and make the economy more productive, it will remove restrictions on companies' behavior. Under deregulation, industries such as airlines or telephone services are allowed to make their own decisions on prices and markets, regardless of the effect on consumers. Deregulation ensures a Darwinian economic environment where only the strongest companies survive.

Derivative. Some securities in the world economy get their value from other securities. An option to buy a stock, for example, goes up in value when the stock's value goes up. A derivative is any financial instrument that derives its value from another financial instrument. Other examples of derivatives are stock index futures, interest rate futures, and options on futures.

Devaluation. A currency will decline in value on the international markets when speculators and traders see an opportunity to buy a stronger currency in its place. Sometimes a government tries to support the value of its currency by buying large quantities, keeping its prices up on the world markets. If it becomes apparent that the market forces are stronger than the government's support, a devaluation will be announced: the government chooses a new, more sustainable level at which to support its currency.

Diminishing returns. The first part in production or consumption is always more rewarding than the end. A hungry consumer, for example, will be less willing to pay as much for a second or third piece of expensive cheesecake. In a factory, new machinery is also subject to the laws of diminishing returns: when the first machines are installed, productivity usually increases rapidly. When additional machines are installed, productivity still increases, but not as quickly.

Discount rate. The interest rate that central banks charge for loans to banks and other financial institutions is called the discount rate. It is usually regarded as a benchmark, because its movement gives an accurate indication of the direction of the credit market as a whole. In the United States, the discount rate is what the Federal Reserve charges banks that borrow from it. This is not to be confused with "Fed Funds," which is the rate banks in the United States charge each other for overnight loans.

Disinflation. Negative inflation is an almost impossible dream for most governments and economists. Since most workers would never accept a lower nominal salary from one year to the next, disinflation, a decline in prices, rarely occurs.

Dividend. A cash payment to a company's shareholders is called a dividend. When a company makes a profit, it has two choices: it can pay the money directly to the shareholders, or it can reinvest the money into the company. In both cases, the shareholder usually benefits. What is not paid as a dividend increases the value of the company, and the share price usually rises accordingly. Dividends can also be in the form of stock or other securities.

Division of labor. Dividing up the jobs in an economy—using, for example, a butcher, a baker, and a candlestick maker— ensures that each job gets done more efficiently. Since no one person can effectively produce everything needed, work is divided among workers of different skills. All modern countries are based on the principle of division of labor.

Dow Jones Industrial Average. The Dow Jones Industrial Average is a summary of the stock prices of thirty of America's premier companies. The average is the most watched indicator of the direction of the U.S. stock market. Some Dow Jones blue-chip stocks are: IBM, AT&T, and General Motors.

Dumping. The sale of goods or services at a price below cost is called dumping. This dubious business practice is used by powerful manufacturers to capture a market. The goal is to drive all competitors out of business and then increase prices at will.

Earnings. A company's earnings are sometimes referred to as profit. Earnings, the proverbial bottom line, are what remains after all the expenses have been deducted from revenue. Earnings are also called net income.

Econometrics. The scientific use of statistics and formulas to develop economic theories is called econometrics. Econometricians use complex mathematical models to simulate real-life situations and test the effect on an economy of changes in such factors as interest rates, taxes, and investment.

Economies of scale. "Many hands make light work." Economies of scale refer to the advantages of making many of the same thing at one time. Henry Ford's first automobile assembly lines used this idea of mass production to produce large quantities of Model T's at an affordable price. Increased production allows the initial costs of investment to be quickly recovered and each unit is produced more efficiently.

ECU. The European Currency Unit was invented by Europe's common market to provide a single unit of value to facilitate accounts. The value of the ECU is determined by the values of currencies from the different European Union countries.

Elasticity. The measure of how much something will change, or stretch, given a certain situation, is called elasticity. In economics, the term is commonly used to describe the behavior of consumers and producers. Elasticity of demand, for example, tells us how much the demand for a product will change given a change in its price. A shopper with high elasticity of demand will rush out and buy a product as soon as it goes on sale.

Equilibrium. Classical economics is based on the theory that all forces in an economy will move toward an equilibrium. When the price of a product is too high, few people will buy it. In order to make a lot of sales, the producer will have to lower the price, bringing the supply into an equilibrium with demand. Equilibriums exist for savings, investment, employment, and inflation.

Equity. Equity means ownership. A stockholder has equity in a company just as a homeowner has equity in a house. On a company's balance sheet, the equity section describes the share of a company that belongs to the shareholders, after liabilities have been deducted from assets. A company's net worth, its assets minus its liabilities, is called stockholders' equity.

Eurodollar. A "currency abroad," Eurodollars are U.S. dollars held in bank accounts outside the United States. The term was invented when big holders of dollars, the Soviet Union especially, opened bank accounts in London to keep their holdings out of the control of U.S. authorities. The prefix "Euro" can be applied to any currency held outside its country, anywhere in the world. Japanese yen held in Singapore, for example, are called Euroyen, just as French francs held in a Canadian bank are called Eurofrancs.

Euromarkets. The restriction-free markets for stocks, bonds, and other financial instruments, centered mainly in London, are called Euromarkets. The Eurobond market, for example, has provided an enormous capital market, free from local restrictions, for trading bonds in a wide variety of currencies.

European Union. The United States of Europe, the European Union is the latest version of the "common market" that has united most of the richest and most powerful economies in Europe. The idea of the original "European Economic Community" was to have a customs union with no barriers to trade among the community's members. Eventually, this evolved into a true European union, with common political, social and economic policies.

Ex. To describe bonds or stocks for which the warrants or dividends have been removed, the word *ex*, from the Latin for "without," is used. A stock sold "ex," for example, has already paid its dividends to the previous owner.

Exchange rates. The value of currencies worldwide is provided by exchange rates. A currency, like any other commodity, is worth only what people will pay for it. Exchange rates tell us how many French francs a U.S. dollar is worth, or how many U.S. dollars a Japanese yen is worth.

Federal Reserve. America's central bank, the Federal Reserve manages the money supply, regulates the banking system, and acts as a lender of last resort. The Federal Reserve answers to no one, except for yearly reports to Congress. It acts independently in keeping the economy on course. The seven members of the Federal Reserve Board are appointed by the president.

Fiscal policy. Fiscal policy refers to a government's use of taxing and spending powers to influence the economy. A government can give the economy a boost by increasing spending, thereby creating jobs and increasing production.

Flight capital. Fearing that economic problems or new laws may make their hard-earned capital worthless, citizens may send money to safe financial havens outside the country. This flight capital sometimes amounts to a large percentage of a country's total wealth. Latin Americans, for example, during times of high inflation at home, buy dollars and send them to bank accounts in Europe and North America, sometimes in defiance of exchange control laws. Often, the more a country tries to keep money from being sent abroad, the more it encourages flight capital.

Floating rate notes (FRNs). Like a home loan with an adjustable interest rate, a floating rate note is a debt security that has its interest rate refixed periodically. Most floating rate notes use LIBOR, the London Interbank Offered Rate, as a reference for determining the interest rate to be paid to the holder. Many banks and investors prefer the price stability of floating rate notes—during a period of fluctuating interest rates, when the prices of fixed-rate bonds can change dramatically, the prices of FRNs remain relatively stable. In order to remain in line with prevailing interest rates, floating rate notes change their interest payment, not their price.

Foreign exchange market. The market that determines the value of currencies around the world is called the foreign exchange market. Currencies trade against one another, as do other commodities, and their prices are quoted in terms of other currencies. Foreign exchange markets, for example, determine how many Japanese yen a Swiss franc is worth, and how many German marks a New Zealand dollar is worth. Foreign exchange trading takes place twenty-four hours a day, usually on bank trading floors that are connected electronically with other banks all over the world.

Forward markets. Traders use forward markets to purchase and sell commodities and financial instruments at a later date. A wheat farmer, for example, could make a forward contract to sell the next year's harvest at today's price. The buyer and the seller both benefit from having the price fixed ahead of the actual delivery. Unlike futures contracts, which are traded on exchanges with fixed prices and dates, forward contracts can be tailor-made to accommodate the needs of different counterparties, such as corporations or growers. Forward markets exist for a wide range of commodities, currencies, securities, and other financial instruments.

Free-market economy. A free-market economy, where the decisions are left up to the market, forces producers to offer consumers the right goods at the right prices. In contrast to a centrally planned economy, where the major economic decisions are made by the state, a free-market economy lets the market decide how much to produce and at which price to sell it.

Friedman, Milton. "Let the markets decide." With followers all over the world, University of Chicago economist Milton Friedman has done more than almost anyone to promote the ideas of free markets. For decades, "Uncle Miltie" has been calling for a worldwide expansion of free trade and capitalism, from Chile to Ukraine. "The freedom to choose" is the goal of Friedman economics: if consumers are allowed to buy what they want and producers are free to sell where they want, the world will be a better place for all.

Futures. Futures are contracts to buy or sell commodities or financial instruments at a fixed price for a fixed time in the future. Because the time and date conform to other contracts, futures can be traded on exchanges. Financial futures were introduced in Chicago in the 1970s, when brokers realized that money and securities, just like other commodities, could be bought and sold for future delivery.

G-7. The "club" of the richest industrial nations, G-7 is the group of seven of the world's largest and wealthiest economies. This select group is made up of the United States, Japan, Germany, France, Britain, Italy, and Canada. They meet periodically to discuss common goals and problems and to coordinate economic policy. The leaders of these "rich" countries usually meet in well-photographed conferences in resorts or capitals of member countries. The European Union and Russia are also usually represented at these meetings.

Game theory. Game theory is a not-so-playful, high-tech way of looking at problems. In theory, all conflicts, including war and trade, can be put into a game-theory formula. The most famous theory looks at wars as a "zero-sum" game where one side's loss is always the other side's gain: the sum of all the wins and losses is said to equal zero. Trade wars, however, can be worse than a zero-sum game because everyone may end up losing. When one side loses the opportunity to sell a useful product on the world markets, it also means a loss for the consumers in the opposing country.

GATT. On the shores of Lake Geneva in Switzerland, the world's major trading nations formed an organization called GATT, the General Agreement on Tariffs and Trade, to monitor and direct trade among its member countries. The goal of GATT was to remove barriers to world trade in goods, services, and ideas. Disputes are now settled by a new entity called the World Trade Organization.

GDP, GNP. Gross domestic product and gross national product measure the total amount of activity in a country's economy. The GDP measures all of a country's domestic production of goods and services. The GNP is a wider measure that includes a country's activities abroad, such as exports and imports and income from foreign operations. Neither GDP nor the GNP tells the whole story, however, because an economy has many unreported activities, such as unpaid housework, voluntary work, environmental destruction, and such illegal activities as drug sales and prostitution. Although the GDP and GNP provide only an estimate of the actual size of an economy, they are the most accurate measures available.

Gearing. Getting more bang for your buck, gearing refers to the amount of debt a company has in relation to its share capital. This is usually called the debt ratio. Just as a bicycle uses a bigger gear on the front sprocket to make the rear wheel go faster, a company can increase its debt to make the stockholders' funds go further. This debt is not free, however, and a highly geared company may get into trouble if high interest payments cannot be paid on time. For most companies, markets look for a gearing of 1 to 1, where debt is no greater than the stockholders' equity.

Glass-Steagall. In Japan, Britain, and the United States, commercial banks are usually not allowed to issue and trade securities, and investment banks are not allowed to take deposits and make loans. This separation of investment banking and commercial banking activities dates from the 1930s in the United States, where the Glass-Steagall Act was passed to protect small bank deposits from being lost in risky securities trading. In Japan, the separation was made law by Article 65. Most European countries, with the exception of Britain, do not see a problem in having a bank undertake both investment and commercial banking activities. French, German, and Swiss "universal" banks can do it all.

Golden parachute. Fearing a hostile takeover of their company, the managers of a company will sometimes incorporate huge guaranteed salaries and bonuses into their own pay packages should they ever be forced out. These golden parachutes are supposed to allow them to land on their feet with their pockets full of money if they find themselves out of a job. This provides a comfort to management, but it is the stockholders who end up footing the bill.

Greenmail. In a takeover or a leveraged buyout, it is sometimes easier to get opponents to change their course of action by offering them a big financial reward. Greenmail refers to the use of financial incentives, such as buying back shares at lucrative prices, to get someone to abandon a hostile takeover attempt.

Hedge. As the name implies, a hedge provides a barrier, a protection from uncertainty. A hedge consists of buying or selling something to protect an investment from unwelcome change in the market. An owner of stocks who thinks the market will go down can hedge by buying put options that give the right to sell at a high price if the market drops. Many investors hedge against inflation by buying real assets, such as real estate or gold.

High net worth individual. The kind of client most banks dream about, a high net worth individual has a lot more disposable assets than liabilities. Banks around the world have discovered the advantages of having these types of clients and have built up private banking operations for them in all of the major financial capitals. In New York, London, Paris, Geneva, Zurich, Luxembourg, Tokyo, and Hong Kong, banks have set up special facilities to cater to the needs of high net worth individuals.

Hot money. Money invested for very short periods, such as overnight deposits, is called hot money. This money comes in as short-term investments, in search of the highest return. It can also leave at a moment's notice, which worries central bankers and finance ministers, who fear the day when the hot money is withdrawn to chase a higher real return somewhere else in the world.

Hyperinflation. Hyperinflation is when prices rise out of control, sometimes at a rate exceeding 1,000 percent per year. It usually occurs in countries with severe economic problems, such as Germany in the 1920s and, most recently, in Latin America.

Import substitution. Import substitution is a government policy that forces consumers to replace imports with locally produced goods and services. This policy has been widely implemented in indebted developing countries in an effort to save precious foreign reserves. The problem is that most countries cannot produce goods and services efficiently without the help of imported goods such as computers and tractors. By forcing companies to buy locally, the whole economy often suffers for lack of imported tools.

Incomes policy. An inflation-control plan that reduces consumers' real disposable income is called incomes policy. It is often used in Third World countries to control rampaging inflation by reducing consumer spending. In order to stabilize prices, incomes policy uses measures such as wage freezes to stabilize consumers' disposable income.

Inflation. Inflation is the percentage increase in prices in an economy, usually measured by an index of consumer prices such as the consumer price index (CPI). Many central bankers see inflation as the world economy's greatest economic evil and make it their policy to control it at all costs, even if it means bringing on an economic recession. Inflation is seen as hurting almost everyone in an economy, including consumers and people on pensions.

Insider trading. A company's insiders are those who have advance knowledge of financial statements and other company secrets. They can benefit from their inside information to trade the company's stocks and options for a profit. In some countries, such as Hong Kong and France, insider trading was not traditionally considered a crime. Insiders were seen as just the first in line for getting the news about a company. This "first come, first served" mentality usually means that insiders start trading before the small investor has a chance. Due to intense international pressure, insider trading has now been made illegal in almost every major market in the world.

Institutional investors. Institutions, such as insurance companies and pension funds, have trillions of dollars, yen, marks, and pounds to invest in the world markets at any given time. Their decisions dwarf most other players in the international markets, including many governments.

Interbank market. The interest that banks charge for loans to other banks is usually the lowest in the market. These interbank rates are then used as a benchmark for other lending. The London Interbank Offered Rate (LIBOR), for example, is used around the world as a base for fixing the interest rate on many loans and securities.

International Development Association (IDA). The IDA is an arm of the World Bank that lends to the world's poorest countries under generous conditions. The IDA and World

Bank are financed by contributions from the governments of wealthy nations.

International Finance Corporation (IFC). The IFC is the arm of the World Bank that makes loans and takes equity stakes in private companies in developing countries.

International Monetary Fund (IMF). The problems of many of the world's debtor countries are so complex that the World Bank and other international lenders will only agree to new loans if the country agrees to an economic austerity plan, usually prescribed by the IMF. The International Monetary Fund was established at the same time as the World Bank, after World War II, to regulate the world's exchange rates, but has now assumed a leading role in restructuring debtor countries' economies and providing short-term loans.

Investment. Economists use the word investment to define the purchase of productive assets such as factories, equipment, houses, and vehicles. Basically, investment powers economic growth.

Investment bank. "Masters of the financial universe," investment banks underwrite new issues of securities, such as stocks and bonds, and trade these securities for their clients, as well as for their own accounts. Since this activity is considered risky, the United States and Japan don't allow investment banks to take deposits. In Britain, investment banks are called merchant banks. In the rest of Europe, "universal banks" are allowed to act as both investment banks and commercial banks. Investment banks are sometimes called securities houses.

Invisible hand. The idea of the invisible hand of the marketplace was formulated by Adam Smith in the eighteenth century to explain how the markets, if left to themselves, will find the most efficient path. The invisible hand refers to the result of millions of profit-seeking consumers and producers making rational decisions, without the interference of state bureaucracies.

Invisible trade. Invisible trade consists of exports and imports of services such as banking and insurance and such other nontangible goods as films and television programs. It also includes interest and dividend payments from foreign investments. One of the most important invisible trades is tourism. Some countries, Germany and Japan, for example, have invisible trade deficits because of all the money their citizens spend abroad while traveling.

Joint venture. A joint venture involves two or more companies joining together, usually to own another company. To compete in difficult foreign markets, many companies prefer joint ventures with a local partner, to take advantage of the local partner's knowledge and skills in the domestic market.

Junk bonds. Companies with low credit ratings often have to issue bonds with high interest rates, in order to get needed capital for expansion or takeovers. These lower-than-investment-grade bonds are often called "junk bonds." The investment banks that issue them prefer to call them high-yield securities.

Keiretsu. Keiretsu is the Japanese word describing the tightly organized system of interlocking corporations with multiple layers of middlemen and brand-loyal retailers that effectively allows Japan to limit imports of foreign products.

Keynesian economics. John Maynard Keynes, a British economist, was one of the world's most influential figures during the Great Depression. His ideas on using government spending to combat economic recession contributed to one of the most important advances in modern economics. Keynesian economics relies on the use of government spending to control the economy. Basically, it calls for overspending, with deficits, during times of economic depression and under-spending, with surpluses, during times of too-rapid economic growth. Most politicians are easily convinced to use deficit spending to stimulate the economy, but are decidedly un-Keynesian when it comes to spending less during periods of rapid economic growth.

Laffer curve. The Laffer curve relates the reduction of taxes to an increase in economic activity. The idea is simple, and it had many fans in the United States during the early years of the Reagan presidency. By lowering taxes, the government is supposed to free up people to increase economic activity, which would bring in more taxes. The Reagan administration, however, somehow ended up doubling the national debt, something many supply siders did not find amusing.

Laissez faire. A French term, *laissez faire* means "let them do it." It is used to describe the government policy that lets the markets decide what is best. Consumers and producers are expected to come to the right decisions on their own.

Leading economic indicators. The statistics prepared by governments to plot the course of future economic activity are called leading economic indicators. They track such things as retail sales, industrial output, housing starts, and financial activity. Leading economic indicators tell us where the economy is going. The statistics that tell us where the economy has been, such as unemployment figures, are called lagging economic indicators.

Letter of credit. In international trade, a letter of credit is used by an importer to provide a guarantee that funds are available to pay for goods sent abroad. A supplier will usually only ship the goods when a reputable bank has provided the necessary letter of credit.

Leveraged buyout. A leveraged buyout uses borrowed money to take over a company. The buyer puts up a small amount of capital and uses huge amounts of debt to buy a company, often over the protests of the company's management. Leveraged buyouts are supposed to make everyone happy: the bondholders, the stockholders, the new owners, and the investment banks who get big fees for their advice. The only problem is that with so much debt, highly leveraged companies have to struggle to meet the enormous interest payments, and sometimes they go bankrupt.

Liabilities. A liability is a debt or other anticipated obligation. On a balance sheet, liabilities are on the right side. They balance the assets listed on the left side. The amount by which assets exceed liabilities is called stockholders' equity. Current liabilities are those that have to be paid off in twelve months or less. Any longer liability is called long-term debt.

Liquidity. Liquidity means a ready supply of funds. On a company's balance sheet, liquidity is a measure of the company's ability to come up with the cash to pay its debts. In a nation's money supply, liquidity refers to the funds injected and drained by the central bank. In the securities market, a bond is said to be liquid if it can be easily traded in large sizes with little effect on the price.

Lombard Rate. The interest rate that central banks such as Germany's Bundesbank charge on collateralized loans to banks is called the Lombard Rate. The banks borrowing the money usually put up government bonds as collateral to receive the preferential Lombard Rates. The name is based on Europe's early bankers, who, more often than not, came from Lombardia, the northern Italian region around Milan.

Macroeconomics. Macroeconomics, the "big picture," is the study of an economy's aggregate factors, such as growth, unemployment, inflation, and government spending. The other side of the economy, the "small picture" of individuals and firms, is called microeconomics.

Margin. Most brokers allow clients to open a margin account to purchase more securities than their cash will allow. The broker then lends the investor money to buy stocks and other financial instruments, which are then used as collateral for the loans. The investor pays interest on this borrowed money. If the value of the securities drops below a certain level, the investor will be asked to put in more money or sell the securities. This moment of truth is referred to as a margin call.

Marginal analysis. The study of behavior at the edges, or how people or firms behave when given the option of having "one more" of something, is called marginal analysis. The additional "one thin wafer," for example, is not as appetizing immediately after the consumption of a huge meal. There is a diminishing return, as more is consumed or saved or spent or earned. Marginal propensity to consume, like other marginal propensities, refers to how much the next good or action is worth. And the next one after that.

Market-maker. "Bid, 25—offer, 26. What do you wanna do? You wanna buy or you wanna sell?" A market-maker will make a two-way price for almost anything. For most securities—such as stocks and bonds—the price at which the market-maker buys is called a bid. It is always lower than the sell price, also called an offer or asked price. The market-maker makes money on the spread, buying low and selling higher the whole day long.

Marx, Karl. "The father of communism." The German economic philosopher and sociologist Karl Marx wrote the first major work on communism, Das Kapital. In it, he foresaw the demise of capitalism and the creation of a socialist economic system based on the philosophy of "from each according to his abilities, to each according to his needs." Marx's pessimistic view of capitalism was based on the terrible inequities he saw in England in the nineteenth century. Ironically, his "communist" revolution did not occur in the industrialized West as he expected, but in rural Russia where it was eventually deformed by the excesses of the Stalin regime.

Mean, median. The terms mean and median are often confused. The simple average is called the mean. This is the "average" school children learn, adding up a list of numbers and dividing the total by the number of items. This is used for most economic calculations such as average income. Sometimes, however, it is useful to look at the way figures are distributed. Like a highway median strip, in a series of numbers, the median is the point at which 50 percent of the numbers are higher and 50 percent are lower.

Mercantilism. The economic policy of using trade surpluses to accumulate wealth and power is called mercantilism. It emphasizes exports over imports. A mercantilist economy aims to produce goods for export instead of domestic consumption. A mercantilist country, such as Japan in the 1980s, ends up with fewer goods for its consumers but with a high level of savings and international investment.

Merchant banking. The term merchant banking is used to describe the practice whereby a securities house invests its own money in its clients' products. This can lead to serious losses for investment banks if their clients' bonds and stocks go down in value.

Mergers and acquisitions. The activity of buying, selling, or joining companies together is referred to as mergers and acquisitions. Much M&A activity involves buying undervalued companies, then merging them with other existing operations or selling off parts to other investors.

Microeconomics. The study of an economy's individuals and firms is called microeconomics. It is the opposite of macroeconomics, which looks at the big picture. Microeconomics, like a microscope, looks at the smaller things, such as the behavior of individuals and how firms make their decisions under various economic conditions.

Monetarism. The economic theory based on the belief that changes in the money supply can control economic growth is called monetarism. Monetarists believe that inflation can best be controlled by reducing the money supply. When the economy appears to be overheating, for example, the central bank can reduce the money supply, which increases interest rates and slows the economy.

Money market. Money markets consist of all the trade in the world's short-term investments. This includes overnight deposits such as interbank deposits, Treasury bills, or fiduciary deposits. In these short-term borrowing and lending operations, money is bought and sold at a price: its interest rate.

Money supply. A country's money supply has many different components, ranging from coins and notes to deposits in savings accounts. The money supply most talked about is called M1, which consists of all notes and coins in circulation and money in bank accounts. This includes checking accounts and other demand accounts that can be withdrawn at a moment's notice.

Monopoly. A monopoly is complete control of one sector of production within an economy. The sole producer of a good can exploit a monopoly to raise prices almost without limit. There are very few real monopolies. Consumers usually find an alternative. The OPEC oil producers thought they had a near monopoly in the 1970s when they dramatically raised oil prices, but many consumers found alternate sources of energy. Antitrust laws are used to restrict monopolies in most countries.

Moody's. Moody's is one of the world's largest credit ratings services. It provides an up-to-date analysis of the financial health of companies, countries and other borrowers in the world economy. Moody's stamp of top quality, "AAA," is awarded only to the world's most creditworthy borrowers, such as Japan, the United States, or Switzerland.

Most favored nation. The most preferential treatment a country can give to its trading partners is to remove barriers to trade, such as tariffs and subsidies. Many countries, such as the United States, have a rule that the "most favored" nations are given the same access to the home market. Most favored nation status doesn't mean that there are no barriers to trade, it only means that no other country has any better terms.

Multilateral trade agreements. When several trading partners agree on a common trade policy, consumers are usually better off. Multilateral trade agreements, often made under the guidance of the General Agreement on Tariffs and Trade (GATT), usually try to remove barriers to trade. The North American Free Trade Agreement (NAFTA) is one of the world's most successful examples of a multilateral trade agreement.

Multinationals. A company with operations in different countries is called a multinational. Once scorned by the developing world as symbols of "capitalist imperialism," multinationals are now courted by most countries, to bring needed capital and jobs. The elimination of trade barriers has made it possible for a company to market a product in several countries at the same time.

Mutual fund. A mutual fund is a collection of bonds or stocks sold to investors as a single investment. This allows investors to avoid risking all of their money on a single company. Each share in a mutual fund is part of a diversified portfolio. Mutual funds are especially appropriate for international investments where information on foreign companies and markets is not easily accessible to the individual investor.

NAFTA. The North American Free Trade Agreement first came into force in 1994, opening up the borders of Canada, the United States, and Mexico to almost limitless trade. The long-term goal in setting up NAFTA was to remove barriers to trade from Alaska to Argentina. NAFTA concentrates on removing internal barriers to trade and does not attempt, as the European Union's common market strategy does, to restrict imports from outside the trading block.

Net assets. What a company really "owns," net assets are what is left when a company's liabilities are subtracted from its assets. Stockholders regard net assets as their share of the company, also called shareholders' equity.

Newly Industrialized Countries (NICs). The Newly Industrialized Countries are a select group of Third World economies seen to be well on their way to joining the ranks of the "developed" nations. Most lists of the Newly Industrialized Countries include Brazil, Israel, Hong Kong, Mexico, Singapore, South Africa, South Korea, Taiwan, and Thailand.

Offshore banking. Offshore banking refers to all those banking activities that are free of domestic restrictions and regulations. To compete with traditional offshore banking centers such as the Bahamas and the Cayman Islands, traditional banking centers like New York have set up facilities to cater to the needs of clients interested in putting their money into tax-free accounts. Other offshore banking centers can be found in London, Luxembourg, Singapore, and Hong Kong.

Open market operations. Central banks use open market operations to buy and sell securities. This has the effect of controlling the money supply, because money held at central banks, such as the U.S. Federal Reserve, is not considered part of the money supply. When central bank money is used to buy securities on the open market, the money supply is increased. Alternatively, when central banks sell securities on the open market, the money supply is reduced by the amount paid into the central banks' vaults. Most securities bought and sold in open market operations are government bonds.

OPEC. The Organization of Petroleum Exporting Countries (OPEC) was established in 1960 to coordinate the policies of most of the world's oil producers. This oil producers' "club" includes Saudi Arabia, Iran, Iraq, Kuwait, the United Arab Emirates, Qatar, Venezuela, Nigeria, Libya, Indonesia, Algeria, Gabon, and Ecuador.

Over-the-counter (OTC). Over the counter shares usually trade electronically, not on stock exchanges. Smaller companies, often so small that they do not meet the strict financial requirements of the established exchanges, trade mainly on OTC markets. Electronic OTC exchanges include NASDAQ in the United States, the USM (Unlisted Securities Market) in Britain, and the OTC and Tokyo "second section" stock exchanges in Japan.

Par. When a bond sells at 100 percent of its nominal value, it is said to trade at par. For most bonds, par is $1,000. For most fixed-income stocks, par is $100. The price of most bonds, however, does not stay at par. When interest rates rise or fall, the price of a new bond has to rise above par or drop below par to make the bond's return competitive with other bonds in the market.

Per capita. Latin for "per head," per capita can also be translated as "per person." A very useful concept in comparing countries, it puts all total figures on a human scale. It is misleading to look only at a country's total economic figures. Brazil may have a total debt larger than Argentina's, for example, but with a much larger population, Brazil's per capita debt is smaller than that of its less populated neighbor.

Perestroika. Russian for "economic restructuring," perestroika became the buzzword of Mikhail Gorbachev's call for economic reform. The goal was to make the economy more efficient by decentralizing decision making.

Poison pill. When a company wants to defend itself against a hostile takeover, it can undertake to render the company unattractive through a series of financial maneuvers called a poison pill defense. A drastic increase in debt, for example, makes the company less attractive financially. A poison pill defense often succeeds in keeping the company in the hands of the original owners, but they may find that it has irreparably harmed the company they were trying to protect.

Preferred stock. Equity that pays a dividend at a fixed rate is called preferred stock. In many ways, it is more like a bond in that its fixed dividend resembles an interest payment. Preferred stock, as the name implies, is considered senior to common stock, except that it does not ordinarily carry voting rights. If a company goes bankrupt, holders of preferred stock are paid off before those holding common stock.

Primary market. When new bonds and stocks are issued, they are traded in a primary market until they are ready to be treated like other seasoned securities. A primary market for bonds will usually exist until the payment date, when the life of the bond as an interest paying security begins. Primary market trading normally takes place outside established trading exchanges.

Prime rate. The interest that U.S. banks charge their best corporate customers is called the prime rate. This rate will then

be used as a guideline for determining the higher rate that the
bank will charge on loans to riskier customers. This follows
the traditional guideline for bank lending: "low risk, low reward." When the prime rate changes, most other rates are
changed as well.

Principal. The face value of a loan, the amount that has to be repaid to the lender, is called its principal. Someone taking out
a loan agrees to two things: to pay a certain amount of interest
over the life of the loan, in addition to paying back the principal.
The principal on some loans, such as those to poor Third World
countries, may never be paid back at all. In the meantime, the
creditors just try to collect as much interest as they can.

Private placement. A private placement is an issue of new equity
or debt securities that is too small to be treated as a public
placement. There are fewer reporting requirements on private placements, and the bonds are sometimes not traded on
the open market. The securities issued in a private placement
are often sold to a small group of institutional investors.

Privatization. A government's "going out of business" sale, privatization is the sale of government-owned companies. Usually inefficient, state-owned companies are often drains on
government resources. When the government decides that its
companies can be run more efficiently in the private sector, it
sells its share in the company to private investors.

Productivity. "Output per capita," productivity compares the
amount of goods or services produced to the amount of people, capital, or land used in the production process. When
machines are used to do the jobs people once performed,
labor productivity usually increases. Basically, when people
work more efficiently, labor productivity goes up, because
more goods are produced by the same amount of people.

Purchasing power parity (PPP). The cost of an average "basket"
of goods and services in a country can serve as a basis for

comparing the value of different countries' currencies. It is often useful to look at a currency's real purchasing power, not the official exchange rate, to compare its value to other currencies in the world economy. For example, the yen's value on the foreign exchange market tells us how many yen can be bought for a hundred U.S. dollars, but it does not tell us what those yen will really buy in Tokyo. PPP allows us to see what each currency can buy in real terms, providing an "alternate" exchange rate.

Quota. A quota is a limit on the quantity of a good that may be imported over a certain period. A government unwilling to open its borders to free trade will set a quota on imported goods, to protect local producers who are not efficient enough to compete on world markets. The result is often a decline in the standard of living, as quality foreign goods are kept from the domestic consumers.

Rational expectations. Much of modern economics is based on the theory of rational expectations, the belief that people, when armed with all the available information, will act logically. Unfortunately, many consumers and producers do not always act rationally, and the theory of rational expectations is flawed.

Real values. Values that have been adjusted for inflation are referred to as real values. In inflationary times, prices often go up so quickly that it is difficult to compare one nominal value to another. By adjusting all statistics for inflation, it is possible to compare their "real" values.

Receivables. "Counting your chickens before they're hatched." On a balance sheet, something owed to the company is considered to be an asset even before it is actually paid. These assets are called receivables. When receivables are paid, they become current assets.

Recession. A recession is a prolonged economic slowdown. The world economy has become so interconnected that an economic recession in one country will often spread to the rest. The first signs of a recession are usually a decline in economic indicators such as housing starts and retail sales. When a country enters a full-blown recession, unemployment rises sharply and interest rates usually decline.

Repurchase agreements. The purchase of bonds with the agreement to sell them back at a certain date in the future is called a repurchase agreement. The terms of a "repo," as repurchase agreements are called in the market, are fixed in advance. Like a short-term deposit, the buyer holds the bonds for only a relatively short time. Central banks, such as the U.S. Federal Reserve or Germany's Bundesbank, use repurchase agreements to inject money into, or remove it from, the economy. When traders see the "Fed" doing repos, they often expect a decline in interest rates, so they rush out to buy bonds.

Rescheduling. When a customer owes the bank a small amount of money and can't pay, the customer is in trouble. When a customer owes the bank a lot of money and can't pay, the bank is in trouble. When confronted with problem borrowers who can't immediately repay their loans, creditor banks sometimes reschedule the loans to give them time to come up with the money. Rescheduling has become a popular way to deal with problem loans to Third World countries because it allows banks and borrowers to avoid admitting that the loans may never be paid off.

Savings. Savings is income that is not spent. When consumers only spend a part of their income, the rest is put aside, usually in banks, where it can be lent for other uses. In an economy, a high savings rate means more money to invest in productive activities such as new factories or businesses.

Savings and Loan (S&L). Savings and Loans are financial institutions that use depositors' money to make loans, primarily to purchase real estate such as homes and office buildings. Deposits are principally from local consumers.

Securities. Worth more than the paper they are printed on, a security is any financial instrument that represents something of value. In international finance, securities are such things as stocks, bonds, notes, and certificates of deposit. Even a written IOU is a security: it states that the holder of the paper is entitled to something of value, usually money. Banks can also securitize their assets, which means, for example, turning loans and mortgages into pieces of paper that can be negotiated on the world markets.

Short selling. In most of the world's markets, investors are allowed to sell stock or other securities they do not own, as long as they agree to provide the securities at some time in the future. This practice is called short selling. Most short sellers borrow the shares from their brokers. A typical short seller is an investor who believes that a stock's price will go down, and who wants to profit from this decline in prices by selling a security early. Short sellers "cover" their short positions by buying the securities after the price has declined.

Smith, Adam. The father of modern economics, Adam Smith was an enlightened eighteenth-century Scotsman who believed that the markets could take care of themselves. He introduced the world to such terms as invisible hand of the marketplace and division of labor. His book, The Wealth of Nations, provided the foundation for the capitalist economic system.

Socialism. The term socialism refers to a wide variety of political/economic systems that attempt to provide an equitable distribution of wealth. There are many free-market socialist countries, in Europe, for example, where capitalism thrives within a socialist framework. Paris, for example, did not stop being a thriving, elegant capital just because the French elected a socialist government. The term "socialism" is often confusing, because it refers both to a form of government and to an economic system.

Special Drawing Right (SDR). A type of money created by the International Monetary Fund as an alternative to gold or other currencies such as the U.S. dollar is called "special drawing rights." These SDRs are used to keep accounts and make payments within the IMF framework. Many countries have begun to use SDRs as a reserve currency. The value of an SDR is based on a basket of several major currencies, such as the U.S. dollar, the Japanese yen, and the German mark.

Speculation. A speculator deals in the market for the simple purpose of making money. In contrast to hedgers and arbitragers, a speculator wants to benefit from the rise or fall of a particular commodity, currency, or security. Speculators think they know something the rest of the market has not yet figured out, and they act on it.

Spot market. A trade executed for immediate delivery and payment is called a spot trade. The alternative to spot trading is to buy or sell in the forward or futures markets, where trades are executed at various prices for delivery and payment sometime in the future.

Stagflation. Where economic stagnation meets inflation, an economy with high inflation and low growth is said to experience stagflation. This phenomenon rarely occurs, because inflation is usually the product of a booming economy, not one in stagnation. Stagflation is a worst-of-both-worlds scenario. It usually occurs when inflationary pressures are so strong that even an economic downturn is unable to quell the pressure toward rising prices.

Standard & Poor's (S&P). One of the world's biggest ratings agencies, Standard & Poor's looks carefully at a company's books, or at a country's financial situation, and makes a judgment. If the company or country is perceived as having an excellent chance of paying back its debts, it is given a AAA rating.

Stock. Stock is ownership in a company. It is represented by units of ownership called shares. A stockholder, also called a shareholder or shareowner, has a claim to the earnings and assets of a company. The company's management is employed by the stockholders to run the company. If a profit is made, it is either distributed as a dividend to the stockholders or reinvested in the company, increasing the assets owned by the stockholders. The word stock is also used to describe a company's inventories.

Stockholders' equity. Stockholders' equity, also called shareholders' equity, is a company's assets minus its liabilities. Basically, if a company were to use its assets to pay off all of its debts, whatever would be left is called stockholders' equity. Stockholders' equity is also called net worth.

Subsidy. A government payment to a business, allowing it to compete with foreign products, is called a subsidy. Most subsidies are criticized as a waste of taxpayers' money because, essentially, they reward inefficiency. In many countries, inefficiently run industries, such as steel producers and airlines, could not survive without government subsidies.

Supply side. Supply side economics is based on the view that producers can stimulate economic growth better than governments. By providing companies and individuals with tax breaks and reduced regulations, a supply side government encourages companies to increase production. The idea is that this increase in production will "trickle down" to individuals through increased employment and spending. Supply side economics is meant to provide an alternative to "demand side" economic systems where governments pump money into the economy through generous spending programs.

Surplus. A surplus occurs when more is coming in than going out. In a trade surplus, more money is flowing in from exports than is flowing out to pay for imports. A government surplus occurs when tax receipts exceed expenditures.

Synergy. "You scratch my back and I'll scratch yours." Synergy is the combining of skills for mutual gain. In trade, synergy refers to the benefits to the world economy of letting countries export those goods and services that they produce most efficiently. Synergy allows each country to be better off by trading its goods and services around the world.

Takeover. A takeover involves controlling enough shares to take command of a company. In a leveraged buyout, for example, a company with a healthy balance sheet and undervalued assets is targeted by arbitragers with large amounts of borrowed money. After gaining control, the takeover group restructures the company and sells off undervalued assets in order to pay off the debt acquired in the takeover.

Tangible net worth. Being discriminating about assets, tangible net worth is an accounting tool that evaluates a company by looking at only its tangible assets and its liabilities. When calculating a company's tangible net worth, all of the nontangible assets, such as goodwill and brand names, are removed from the balance sheet. A brand name, for example, is an intangible asset because, although it can be bought and sold, it does not represent any clearly quantifiable value, such as office buildings or land.

Tariffs. A tariff is a tax on imports. Tariffs are trade barriers that a country uses to make imports from other countries more expensive. Although most governments say their goal is free trade, they often let themselves be convinced by local companies that protection is necessary to save jobs at home. Essentially, tariffs reduce the competition from lower-priced and often higher-quality foreign made products. Unfortunately, it is often the consumers who have to pay the cost of higher priced domestic products protected by tariffs.

Tax haven. A tax haven is a country, often a small nation with little local industry, where companies and individuals are allowed to set up with little or no taxes on income and profit. Many companies prefer to set up some sort of subsidiary in tax havens, such as the Bahamas or the Cayman Islands, to reduce their tax burdens. Individuals, like international tennis stars, often move their official residence to such tax havens as Monaco, for the same reason.

Third World. The world's poor and developing countries are referred to as the Third World. Some Third World countries are doing so well that they are poised to join the ranks of the developed industrialized countries. These lucky few are called Newly Industrialized Countries, or NICs. The rest are struggling to increase economic production to allow their growing populations to enjoy a minimum of economic prosperity. Those countries that are so poor that they are not developing at all are sometimes called "Fourth World" countries.

Trade balance, balance of trade. A country's trade balance, or balance of trade, is not really a balance at all: it is merely a measure of the total exports and imports of merchandise. Generally, the term trade balance does not include the trade in services and investments that make up the country's wider measure of trade, the current account.

Unemployment. The percentage of an economy's work force that is looking for a job is defined as "unemployment." Economists and politicians use this figure to judge how well an economy is working. Some unemployment statistics also include those people out of work who are not looking for a job. Every economy needs a certain amount of unemployment, to keep a steady supply of people ready to move to a new job when it opens up.

Unilateral trade restrictions. A decision by a country to impose trade barriers without prior agreement with its partners is called a unilateral trade restriction. These singlehandedly imposed trade barriers, usually tariffs and quotas, often provoke retaliation by unilateral trade restrictions in other countries, and before long a trade war is under way.

Value added tax (VAT). A tax applied at each stage of production is called a value added tax. Every time the product's value is increased, a tax on the added value has to be paid. In contrast to a sales tax, which is paid by the consumer at the point of sale, a value added tax is paid by all parties in the production process. VAT is used in almost all modern industrial economies to distribute the tax burden more evenly between producers and consumers.

Velocity. Economists use the word velocity to describe a country's economic activity in relation to its money supply. This "speed of money" refers to the amount of economic activity that takes place with a limited amount of money in the economy. When a country can produce a high GNP on a small money supply, it is said to have a high velocity of circulation.

Venture capital. Money invested in companies with a potential for rapid growth is called venture capital. Start-up companies interested in rapid growth usually turn to venture capital funds to obtain the needed capital for high-risk ventures.

Volatility. The movement of a price or another measure over a given time is called its volatility. This measure looks at both frequency of movement and amount of movement. A stock, for example, that moves often and widely in any direction is said to be highly volatile. The volatility of stocks, bonds, commodities, and indexes is a major factor in determining their price. Stock investors pay less for a highly volatile stock because it implies greater risk.

Wage-price spiral. A wage-price spiral consists of a rapid growth of inflation resulting from a vicious circle of wage increases followed by price increases and so on. Like the proverbial chicken and egg, it is difficult to determine which came first, and even more difficult to find a way to break the inflationary wage-price spiral.

Warrant. A warrant gives the holder a certain right, usually to buy a company's stock. Most warrants are issued with bonds or common stock and give the holder the right to purchase additional stock at a favorable price. Because they are issued in limited amounts, warrants are different from options, which are supplied according to demand.

Withholding tax. A withholding tax is deducted at the time an income is received. In most countries, stock dividends and bond interest payments are subject to a withholding tax. This allows the tax authorities to receive their money before it goes into the pocket of the investor.

World Trade Organization. Set up to supplement the trade liberalization of GATT, the General Agreement on Tariffs and Trade, the World Trade Organization is a global tribunal to settle trade disputes. Based in Geneva, Switzerland, the WTO is made up of almost all of GATT's former member countries. It cannot change any country's internal laws, but can authorize trade sanctions against any country found to be in violation of GATT's agreement to open up borders to free trade.

Yield. "Many happy returns!" Yield is the return on an investment, stated in percentage terms. When a ten-year bond is said to be yielding 8 percent, the purchaser will receive a return of 8 percent per year until maturity. In order to compare different investments with different interest rates, prices, and maturities, it is essential to calculate their annual percentage return—their yield. Yields can be applied to almost any investment in the world economy.